PENGUIN BUSINESS
THE PRACTICAL MBA

Sandeep Das is a business storyteller and global foresight lead (emerging countries) for Mars Wrigley. An MBA from IIM Bangalore, Sandeep has held leadership positions across consulting and FMCG industries for over fifteen years. He is a guest faculty at IIM Ahmedabad, IIM Bangalore and IIM Lucknow.

T0282990

PRAISE FOR THE BOOK

'Sandeep has brought to life in his own very unique conversational style, a veritable compendium of hacks to live a more productive and fulfilling life. A definite must-read in today's fast-paced life'

—**Sunit Sinha**, *Managing Director,*
Accenture Strategy

'Have always been a fan of Sandeep's eloquence, now also a fan of his sarcasm. Scintillating writing—a must-read for all millennials out there. This is your definitive guide'

—**Prakash Deep Maheshwari**, *Head,*
Marketing Strategy & Analysis, Netflix

'It's time we acknowledge that millennials talk and learn in a different language. Kudos to Sandeep for stepping up to the challenge of penning a book that not only speaks it but does it with a flourish'

—**Nistha Tripathi**, *Bestselling Author of*
No Shortcuts

'Written in simple, easy-to-understand language, the book will surely keep you gripped'

—**Shweta Rashmi**, *Anchor-cum-Producer at*
CNN-News 18

'This book is a great read for different types of readers—managers, entrepreneurs, students starting off their careers'

—**Dr Anup Krishnamurthy** *(PhD, IIM Bangalore)*,
Associate Professor of Marketing,
St. Joseph's Institute of Management

'Millennials would lap this book up'

—**Benedict Paramanand**, *Founder, Bangalore*
Business Literature Festival

'The book focuses on the very practical aspects of life that are extremely pertinent in the times we all live in'

—**Sandeep Bhalla**, *Partner, Korn Ferry*

'This book will be your bridge to the corporate world'

—**Manbir Kaur**, *Author of* Are You
The Leader You Want To Be?

'This is an incredible package of very powerful career tips for a millennial. The thought-provoking sarcasm makes for an engrossing read throughout'

—**Prateek Gupta**, *Head, Strategy & Business*
Development, Aditya Birla Finance

'Hacks for life and career makes for the perfect book for all confused millennials. The sarcasm and wit make for an easy, yet informative and enjoyable read!'

—**Geetika Srivastava**, *Journalist*

'Sandeep has wittily crafted sound advice for millennials through his humorous narratives. A must-read!'

—**Ashray Siddaiah,** *Senior Category Manager,*
Amazon European Union

'Sandeep's new book offers legit advice to millennials on a variety of topics with a dose of sarcasm thrown in'

—**Madhurranjan Mohaan,** *Tech Lead Manager,*
Google California

'This book is an excellent one-stop shop for key nuggets of business such as digital, gig economy, creativity, hyper-innovation. A must-read'

—**Amit Agarwal,** *Cluster Head, Larsen and Toubro*

The Practical MBA

A Quick Guide to What You Don't Learn at B-Schools

SANDEEP DAS

PENGUIN
BUSINESS

An imprint of Penguin Random House

PENGUIN BUSINESS

Penguin Business is an imprint of the Penguin Random House group of companies
whose addresses can be found at global.penguinrandomhouse.com

Published by Penguin Random House India Pvt. Ltd
4th Floor, Capital Tower 1, MG Road,
Gurugram 122 002, Haryana, India

Penguin
Random House
India

First published as *Hacks for Life and Career* by SAGE Publications India Pvt. Ltd 2021
Published in Penguin Business by Penguin Random House India 2024

Copyright © Sandeep Das 2021

10 9 8 7 6 5 4 3 2 1

The views and opinions expressed in this book are the author's own and the
facts are as reported by him which have been verified to the extent possible,
and the publishers are not in any way liable for the same.

ISBN 9780143461197

Typeset in 11/14 pt Sabon by Fidus Design Pvt. Ltd, Chandigarh
Printed at Replika Press Pvt. Ltd, India

www.penguin.co.in

MIX
Paper | Supporting
responsible forestry
FSC™ C016779

To Mom and Dad for everything
they have done for me

CONTENTS

Acknowledgements xiii

Introduction: So Why Should You Read This Book? xv

How to Get the Most Out of This Book xxi

Part 1 Technology: How Zeros and Ones Are Changing the World! 1

    Chapter 1 Our Future 3

    Chapter 2 Future of the Grocer 7

Part 2 Gurukul: Setting Up the Foundation 11

    Chapter 3 GDP: The Sum of All We Do 13

    Chapter 4 Inflation: The Beast That Erodes Money 17

    Chapter 5 Pricing: What's the Fuss about? 20

    Chapter 6 Elasticity: Am I Really That Sensitive? 26

    Chapter 7 Doing a Brand Manager's Role 30

    Chapter 8 Boring but Necessary Numbers: Part 1 35

    Chapter 9 Boring but Necessary Numbers: Part 2 40

    Chapter 10 Can You Mathematically Answer
                 Why I Am Putting On Weight? 43

    Chapter 11 Is This Industry Attractive? 47

    Chapter 12 Leveraged Buyout: The Educated Gambler! 52

    Chapter 13 Growth Strategy: Selling a Dream 56

    Chapter 14 Game Theory: Selfish or Co-operate? 60

    Chapter 15 Vagaries of the Human Mind 63

    Chapter 16 Understanding the Net Working Capital
                 Concept to Realize How a Business Is Run 67

    Chapter 17 NPV: Focus on the Now 71

    Chapter 18 Financial Statements: The King
                 amongst Kings! 75

Chapter 19 Enterprise Value: How Much Do I Need to Pay to Takeover Apple?........................90

Part 3 Entrepreneurship: Building the Next Big Thing..........93

Chapter 20 Building Your Own Unicorn................................95

Chapter 21 Why Entrepreneurs Fail.....................................101

Chapter 22 Writing a Business Movie Script.........................105

Chapter 23 New-Age Slash Careers.....................................113

Chapter 24 Forecasting the Next Decade.............................116

Part 4 Your Office: Braving the Wilderness of Corporate India..........121

Chapter 25 The *Feku* (The Perennial Bluff Master)...............123

Chapter 26 Our Famed Work Culture..................................127

Chapter 27 Great Ways to Exit Your Current Boss................131

Chapter 28 Appearing Smart in Meetings without Having Any Clue.....................135

Part 5 Water Cooler Talk: The Modern-Day World Trends.................139

Chapter 29 Greatest Financial Crises over the Last Few Decades.....................141

Chapter 30 Overcoming the Demand Slowdown...................147

Chapter 31 Need to Do Everything....................................152

Chapter 32 The Lure of Rural India...................................156

Chapter 33 Minimalism at Work..159

Chapter 34 Chemicals in Good Leaders..............................162

Chapter 35 Selling Cement Like iPhones............................166

Chapter 36 The Art and Science of Creating Analytics Dashboards.....................169

Chapter 37 When in Rome, Do as the Romans Do...............172

Chapter 38 The Mentalist..175

Chapter 39 The Future of Corporate Governance.................179

Part 6 Personal Finance: Managing Your Own Money..........183

Chapter 40 A Fool and His Money Are Soon Parted.............185

Chapter 41 Multiplying Your Money Every Day...................195

Part 7 Industry Primers: Learning the Ropes about Your Likely Jobs ...199

    Chapter 42 FMCG: At the End of the Day, It Is All about Selling Soap 201

    Chapter 43 E-commerce: The Online Everything Store 207

    Chapter 44 Banking: Modern-Day Shylock, Lend and Earn.....................................212

    Chapter 45 Management Consulting: Glitz, Glamour and Drama 217

    Chapter 46 Big Brother: How Does the Indian Government Work? 221

Part 8 Your Career: Getting Your Dream Education and Job 227

    Chapter 47 Getting the Maximum Out of Your Business School 229

    Chapter 48 Getting Your Dream Job in a Business School 234

    Chapter 49 Writing Your Dream Resume 240

    Chapter 50 Excelling in a Group Discussion 244

    Chapter 51 The Slog Overs 247

    Chapter 52 Constructing a High-Profile LinkedIn Page 250

    Chapter 53 The Lure of the International MBA 253

    Chapter 54 Nailing Your Internship...........................257

    Chapter 55 Immediate Life after a Business School 262

    Chapter 56 Self-Sabotaging Social Media Habits 266

Part 9 Happiness: Longing for a Meaningful Life....................................273

    Chapter 57 Why Should You Read Business Books? 275

    Chapter 58 Following a True Calling, Not a Fake Hobby.....280

    Chapter 59 Stress Free and Productive in Times of a Global Crisis 285

    Chapter 60 Learnings from a Trek up to Tiger's Nest 290

    Chapter 61 Finally: 10 Commandments to Leading a Meaningful Life!.................................296

Notes 301

ACKNOWLEDGEMENTS

I have a lot of people to thank for helping me finish my third book and encouraging me along the way. I would like to start by thanking Mom and Dad who have always supported me in whatever I have wanted to do. I would like to thank my editors—Namarita Kathait and Manisha Mathews—for having been extremely patient with me and tolerating all my stupid queries.

In addition, I am profoundly grateful to my professors and colleagues at work who encouraged me along the way. I should add I was quite a nasty student and would ask all sorts of uncomfortable questions to my professors. In hindsight, I am thankful to them for patiently tolerating me. To further clarify, I still ask nasty questions to people around me at work!

A big thank you to the following people who read almost every piece of work, good and bad, I have written over the last few years and gave me their valuable feedback at every point—Dipti Sharma, Priya Jain and Natasha Prakash.

INTRODUCTION: SO... WHY SHOULD YOU READ THIS BOOK?

Well, you may be thinking right now whether you should buy this book or not. You may be reading this chapter to make up your mind. I would recommend you read the next few pages and then make up your mind. Make up your mind to BUY the book.

What is the core issue this book is trying to solve?

As per numerous reports, the majority of management graduates and aspiring management graduates in India are unemployable. For instance, a research study conducted by the Associated Chambers of Commerce & Industry of India (ASSOCHAM) indicates that 93 per cent of management graduates are unemployable in India.* For this book, I ended up speaking to over 100 Chief Experience Officers (CXOs) and heard similar sentiments from them.

I also spoke to a lot of 20-something people. Turns out nobody is listening to their viewpoint. They find traditional management education not in line with the times. Phrases like 'theoretical', 'boring' and 'no applications in the real world' keep coming up again and again.

Traditional management education is expected to fill this gap between what CXOs expect and what management graduates want. However, most of the educational institutions are failing to do so. This mismatch leads to immense dissatisfaction at work, stress, mental health issues, lack of

---

* Roshni Chakrabarty, 'Isn't it staggering that 93% of management graduates in India are unemployable! Link to the study', *India Today*, 6 February 2018, https://www.indiatoday.in/education-today/featurephilia/story/mba-education-problems-328626-2016-07-11.

purpose at work and everything that is wrong with modern careers today.

You may ask why. There are many reasons for this mismatch.

Most business schools do not bring in enough experts from the industry for a real-world perspective. Or their textbooks are stuck in the 1960s or are too theoretical. Or their teaching style is, just for lack of a better word, 'boring'.

This is where this book fits in. To bridge the gap between what corporate leaders need and what you want. Think of this book as a tool to teach you what a top-notch business school will teach you. In about 300 pages. In simple English, in a month or two of reading this book, you will have access to quality management education, which only hundreds can ever dream of!

You may or may not want to do an MBA, but you will need access to quality management education in your 20s.

Also, the chapter names are really cute and may tickle your funny bone. Or maybe not—you will find that out soon.

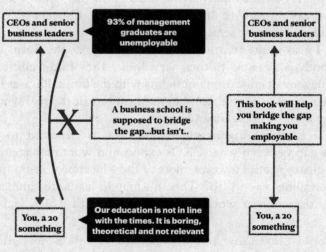

Figure 1: How This Book Bridges the Gap between What You Know and What Industry Leaders Want You to Know

But...Who Is Sandeep Das?

Sandeep Das, the author or me, in case you didn't figure it out, is probably the right person to write this book. I have held leadership positions across consulting and FMCG industries in my 15-year corporate career. I was a director at PwC (PricewaterhouseCoopers) and the global foresight lead for emerging countries for Mars Wrigley.

I am a guest faculty at leading Indian business schools like IIM Ahmedabad, IIM Bangalore and IIM Lucknow. I am a corporate coach with leading corporates like Hindustan Unilever Limited (HUL), the Tata Group, Deloitte, PwC, etc. My MBA is from IIM Bangalore and I have a strategy degree from INSEAD, France.

You may also know me as the author of the bestselling book, *How Business Storytelling Works: Increase Your Influence and Impact.* If you liked that book, you will love this one.

I have seen and heard many of the issues related to the unemployability of management graduates and poor-quality management education play out in front of me.

Hence, I am the right person to author this book!

How Do You Read This Book?

You may be thinking about how to get the most out of this book. Let me simplify this for you. This book is divided into 9 parts and I recommend you read one part every week, thereby helping you finish the book in about 2 months. The book has a repository of brilliant insights and I would recommend you write down the top 3 points you take away after you finish each of the 61 chapters.

Not bad, I would say, if you learn about quality management education by reading for a couple of hours every weekend for 2 months.

Before you move to the next set of chapters, let me give you an overview of what each of the 9 parts in the book has.

Part 1 titled 'Technology: How Zeros and Ones are Changing the World' gives a sense of where the world might be headed in the next few years. If you understand the future, you may understand the present better. Honestly, the future is so complex and fluid that by the time you read this book, the future may be the past!

Part 2 titled 'Gurukul: Setting up the Foundation' explains 17 key concepts that you need to master to understand the world of business well. These concepts have been explained in a layman's fashion so that you can grasp their simplicity and richness. For instance, these concepts can help you explain the following,

How do you understand how much a brand's sales will reduce if you increase the price? Enter Chapter 6 titled 'Elasticity: Am I Really That Sensitive?'

How do you understand the unpredictability of the human brain and how can you use that in your daily lives? Enter Chapter 15 titled 'Vagaries of the Human Mind'

How do you value a firm? How much is Apple worth or how much is your startup venture worth today? Enter Chapter 17 titled 'NPV: Focus on the Now'

Part 3 helps you understand the most glamorous and abused area of the modern world, 'Entrepreneurship'. If you want to build the next big thing, this section helps you understand how to build a profitable unicorn, the risks you should be aware of and the new-age careers that are coming out of the entrepreneurship boom.

Part 4 titled 'Your Office: Braving the Wilderness of Corporate India' tells you how to succeed in an office with politics and bad bosses. I strongly recommend you read Chapter 25 titled 'The *Feku* (The Perennial Bluff Master)'.

You may think I should have considered an alternate career as a stand-up comic after reading this chapter. To be honest, I haven't pursued it till now but may do it in the future.

Part 5 titled 'Water Cooler Talk: The Modern-Day World Trends' speaks about contemporary conversations that are happening in boardrooms across India. For instance, Chapter 32 discusses the infinite potential that is rural India and how you can navigate it to win it. Chapter 36 discusses how you can create beautiful analytics dashboards that are a source of immense value to your business. Read Chapter 37 to understand how you can master the nuances of cross-cultural communication and succeed in a global career.

Part 6 titled 'Personal Finance: Managing your Own Money' builds on the adage, 'a fool and his money are soon parted'. If there is one skill that isn't taught formally today, it is knowledge about money management. This section addresses that must-know skill set. It speaks about the various financial instruments that are available to you and how you can build the optimal portfolio for you depending on the life stage you are at.

Part 7 titled 'Industry Primers: Learning the Ropes about Your Likely Jobs' explores the nuances of the industries you are likely to work in—FMCG, management consulting, e-commerce and banking. Read these chapters to get a sense of what your future is likely to be. This section ends by also telling you how Big Brother—the government—works, how they make money and how they spend money.

Part 8 titled 'Your Career: Getting your Dream Education and Job' helps you get started with your career. For instance, Chapter 47 tells you how you can maximize your MBA. Chapter 52 tells you how you can build a superb brand on LinkedIn. Chapter 54 tells you how you can succeed in your internship.

Part 9 titled 'Happiness: Longing for a Meaningful Life' is the most important section in the book and discusses with you how you can lead a happy, contented life. Not the crap that influencers peddle these days on social media but practical aspects that touch your day-to-day life. The one chapter I particularly encourage you to read is Chapter 61 titled 'Finally: 10 Commandments to Leading a Meaningful Life!'

The name says it all, doesn't it?

Conclusion

In conclusion, hope you enjoy reading this book. I think it may be the most important investment you make in your life. And yes, do tell your friends about it by posting it on your social media pages. No author has been harmed when their readers have advocated their books. Besides, your knowledge gains when you spread it.

Once you are done with this book and like it, please read my other bestselling book, *How Business Storytelling Works: Increase Your Influence and Impact.* That book will teach you business storytelling—the #1 skill you need to succeed in your career going ahead!

HOW TO GET THE MOST OUT OF THIS BOOK

This book has a lot of useful information.

It is consciously structured as a set of chapters under a specific theme. Although it is difficult to absorb everything at one go, I would suggest you read 3–5 chapters in one go and for each chapter you read, write down 3 key points you learnt or took away from that.

If you remember 3 key points per chapter, you will be intellectually richer by 200+ key points by the time you finish the book. It is a damn good deal in my opinion. (If you are more financially inclined, it will cost you about ₹2 per takeaway.)

In terms of time, you should target to finish this book in about 2–3 months if not earlier.

After that, you may go ahead and buy my other 2 books.[1]

TECHNOLOGY

HOW ZEROS AND ONES ARE
CHANGING THE WORLD!

The one aspect that dominates media and business literature is the rise of technology and the devastating impact it will have on our jobs. Words like artificial intelligence, machine learning, natural language processing and their nerdy sisters are thrown around akin to the local *dhobi* smashing our clothes away. While it is difficult for me to generate a view on if we will lose our job this year or if we will have a romantic affair with a robot instead of our spouse, this section will take us through a couple of interesting chapters on how the future of work might look like and how the future of the grocer might look like. Both of these are critical as we will be the direct protagonist for them.

"

*Toyota has announced it will start integrating
Microsoft technology into their vehicles.
It's perfect for the person who wants a car that
crashes every ten minutes.*
Conan O'Brien,
American comedian

*A computer once beat me at chess, but it was
no match for me at kick boxing.*
Emo Philips,
American comedian and actor

"

1

OUR FUTURE

The popular press is filled with notions of how technology advancements (read artificial intelligence, machine learning and their nerdy sisters) will position man and machine at loggerheads competing for the same job.[2] In my opinion, far from the man versus machine impending sci-fi war, machines will end up playing a much bigger 'human' role—a majestic combination of your mom, office mentor, agony aunt, vegetable vendor, domestic help, society matchmaker and so on.

Read on to ascertain how the millennial's life will seem half a decade from today!

Mehak, a 27-year-old Mumbai girl, is a brand manager with a leading FMCG company. Armed with an arts degree from Mumbai University followed with an MBA from IIM, she is living life king-size.

She is up at 6:30 AM sharp to the tune that Google plays in her wristband. Google has adjusted the tune to the level of sunlight and humidity outside along with her quality of sleep the night before. It also suggests the steps she has to cover in the morning during her morning jog. It serves her critical information she can process before she brushes: her fat percentage, nature of impending wrinkles and the quality of her hair!

Prior to stepping out in the morning, Mehak's fridge opens on its own and churns out the right breakfast. It is 'right' because the fridge is smart enough to serve a different meal with the right blend of carbohydrates, nuts and proteins every day. To ensure Mehak's domestic help doesn't pinch from the fridge to glory, it only opens looking at Mehak's early morning face! It has been nearly a decade since Face ID was given birth to!

While running, Mehak's footwear adjusts as per the terrain (Mumbai roads, after all, are not the most runner friendly) and even sends out instructions to her watch and her phone on the stress the foot is undertaking.

It is easy to dress up if you are Mehak. She wears the same 'wearable' shirt every day. Yes, you read it right! It is the same shirt every day. The shirt changes colour and texture automatically. And you don't need to wash and press it. It is 'dust' and 'wrinkle free' in the truest sense of the word.

After she battles her way to office in a 'one-seat cab aggregator', she walks up to her cubicle to breathe in natural air. The glass window in front of her cubicle facing the street automatically adjusts to simulate pleasant weather inside the office with the right amount of sunlight, wind and humidity.

The first thing she has to do is to take 15 interviews for an entry-level position in her team. She requests her 'interviewing bot' to screen the candidates and present her two to three best candidates. She gives the bot clear instructions not to repeat the previous time's experience. An ethical hacker from IIT managed to crack through the interview process (not him, but his parrot) after his trained parrot managed to crack the interview code and successfully made it to the last round!

She keeps chatting with another bot till lunch. She requests her bot to file her expenses. She asks the bot how her boss' mood is. The bot replies 'patchy'. She questions the bot if he fought with his wife. The bot winks at her!

Post lunch, her day seems to take on a more serious note. She asks her bot which promotion she should run for one of her key products during Christmas. The bot replies 'buy one get one'. She is not convinced. She asks for another answer. The bot replies 'flat 50 per cent'. She is moderately pleased.

Meanwhile, her company has sent her a few emails on the various engagement measures her company is tracking for her. The company talks about her company engagement score, her depression index (which has been moving in the right direction in the last two months), her stress index, her posture index, her hairline index (one of the company attached vendors also sent in the designs of the latest wigs), her savings index and so on.

At home, the fridge, after the domestic help has grudgingly left, has automatically asked Amazon to send in replenishments. Bigbasket has been overhearing the conversation between the fridge and Amazon and has sent the same thing at 20 per cent discount, 10 minutes before the Amazon shipment arrived!

During tea, Mehak goes through her Tinder++ app. It is the latest app to be tagged the 'ultimate unicorn' (read $10 bn valuation). It shows a person's original picture minus filters—so if you are fat, you will appear fat! Its astronomical valuations have been attributed to its incredible technology that can actually take a picture without distorting it through exposure, shades, filters, colours and so on.

Her office relationship bot chooses not to converse with her today as her relationship index seems to be improving.

Post work, Mehak decides to try the UberChic 'self-driving cab aggregator'. She boards a 'two-seater' self-driving cab aggregator (she doesn't want to look cheap by booking a 'one-seater' self-driving cab aggregator in front of her colleagues). The cab seems to move effortlessly through the crowded roads in Mumbai till it bangs into something. Not a pole. Not a garbage bin. Not a car. Not a bike. Not a shop. Not a human. Unfortunately, the car bangs into a cow eating at a bakery!

Ouch! Ouch! Ouch!

The cow is tagged with a radio-frequency identification device (RFID) tag. With the impact, the RFID tag of the cow (and the numerous cows in the vicinity) starts beeping viciously. A central alert team is activated. Facebook is tracking status of the cows and marking them safe on their pages. There is panic in the liberal media to ascertain if this is an isolated attack on a cow or a mass technology-enabled attack on all cows.

A few journalists land up. A hundred cops are present at the impact site. Smartphones, sensing commotion outside, start capturing the video at the point of impact.

YouTube is trending. Facebook is trending. Sorry, Instagram is trending. Facebook is for old people! Pinterest is trending. (This is actually a very powerful insight that Facebook is seemingly not being used by the next generation as their preference turns to Instagram. Look at your own friend circle in Facebook and see how many friends of yours less than 25 years of age are active on it.)

While Mehak looks on helplessly expecting her bots to advise her out of the situation, the media is preparing for a vicious debate the next day on whether machines can really do the jobs which men are supposed to!

In conclusion, the above tale is not a figment of imagination. It is closer to reality than you might think it is.

In the next chapter, we look at the local grocer, one of the biggest employment generators and the chief protagonist of the technology revolution.

2

FUTURE OF THE GROCER

Over the last few years, the neighbourhood grocer has had an incredible transformation.[3] Their format, from being unorganized, messy, managed by an underage child has transformed into a neat self-service store with relatively modern amenities including an air conditioner, neat display racks and an open store format where consumers choose on their own. The quality of merchandising, or shelf decoration, has rapidly evolved from torn danglers to acrylic shelf strips. Electronic payment systems are becoming the norm with some even piloting consumer loyalty programs!

This dramatic change has been necessitated by the rapidly growing modern trade channel and the rise, although on a small base, of e-commerce. Operating margins in grocery retail are wafer thin and any threat to consumers shifting to another channel is always scary. In my opinion, the single biggest change has been the phenomenal success of DMart. Their simplistic formats, incredible pricing and vast collection has led to consumers thronging their stores akin to a jaw-dropping Zara sale every day!

With modern trade expected to continue to show disproportionate growth, especially in packaged groceries and Amazon looking to enter this space, the neighbourhood grocer, primarily the larger ones, are bound to have a jaw-dropping transformation.

Read on for what your local grocery store might look like in a decade!

Can I Speak to Someone, Please?

While many believe the experiment by Amazon (in Seattle and Chicago) and Microsoft of a manless and cashless store is equivalent to a science fiction project, it is an idea whose time has come even in developing countries. It is known that the single biggest pain point in any form of retail, unorganized and organized, is waiting time at billing counters. With massive 4G penetration in urban areas and a smartphone comfortable consumer base, it is not long before your neighbourhood grocer might pilot a manless store. Who knows, your billing might be linked to your mobile wallet linked to your Aadhar! Or even to your registered face ID without make-up! That might be touchy, isn't it?

We Love Inception, Show Us What Is a Level Beneath

It is evident that technology will play a huge role in the transformation journey of large grocers. In addition to a manless store, the second pillar of technological intervention is going to be augmented reality. For instance, when you take your smartphone and scan the barcode of a Patanjali toothpaste, your phone opens an app which provides information about the ingredients, stories about where it was sourced from, how eco-friendly it is, necessary videos differentiating the product from its competition and sample testimonials from others who have used it. In short, bringing a boring regular everyday product to five-dimensional life. With health and wellness expected to be a massive spend of consumer wallet in the next decade, augmented reality is bound to enter your neighbourhood store!

Look at Me, Let Me Drive You to My Shelf

The biggest transformation that has occurred over the last few years and is bound to occur over the next decade is in in-store activations. With consumers being spoilt for products while companies and channels compete for their share of wallet, in-store activations have come a long way. And they are expected to leapfrog in quality of interaction in the years to come!

While an experience akin to the movie *Minority Report*, where the interaction is customized basis the Iris of the consumer is far way—interactive walls, live sampling counters, competent product promotion workforce, also called promoters in regular parlance, are bound to enter your neighbourhood grocer.

The only constraint that exists is that real estate in India will continue to be very expensive and hence miniature versions of consumer engagement will flourish rather than life-sized versions in the developed world.

Let Me Be Your Prince Charming and Drive You Around

It is a no-brainer that smartphones will drive everything in the future from shopping to eating to hiring for jobs. It is expected to be no different for your neighbourhood grocer. Smartphone apps will significantly assist in simplifying grocery shopping. For instance, when a consumer enters a store, her smartphone might recommend what she should buy and the pathway inside the store she can take for ease of shopping. There is a possibility of her picking up her shipment right then or asking a delivery executive at the store to drop it off at her place. All these fancy figments of imagination will be basis her historical purchase and analysis of heat maps, density of people at various places, inside the store.

Let Us Make a Rag Tag Coalition

Like most spheres in life, when there is an overarching enemy, everyone else seems to combine to form a rag tag coalition. Pick up today's newspaper and this theme might resonate very strongly.

With DMart being the blue-eyed boy among grocery shoppers and other grocers eyeing it with seething rage, it is only a matter of time that a lot of them come to a common platform to offer scale benefits to their consumers. They can either negotiate together with their suppliers to offer better margins to their consumers or have consumer loyalty programs across their rag tag coalition. Or they might partner with Amazon to use their store as a hub for delivery!

In conclusion, the neighbourhood grocer, at least the larger ones, are bound to change significantly over the next decade. It is anybody's guess on the scale of transformation that is bound to occur. For all you know, your existing grocer format might be seen as history in a 2025 movie! Or there might still be a DMart that might ignore everything else and just keep giving the best prices that drive consumers crazy!

GURUKUL

SETTING UP THE FOUNDATION

There are a lot of things that are taught in institutes of higher education, some useful in the real world, most of them not. A curriculum that seemingly ignores the real world leads to discontent at the workplace and leads to poor technical capabilities to succeed in a professional sphere. This section tries to highlight two dozen concepts which the real world requires most of the time.

Sell a man a fish, he eats for a day.
Teach a man to fish, you ruin a wonderful
business opportunity.
Karl Marx
ironically, a great advocate
of Communism

The light at the end of the tunnel has
been turned off due to budget cuts.
Unknown
(It isn't me!)

3 | GDP: THE SUM OF ALL WE DO

One of the pivotal concepts in macroeconomics is the notion of gross domestic product (GDP).

What Does This Exotic Term Mean?

GDP in popular parlance is a measure of the entire output of a country. Every individual or a company can produce a good (e.g., toothpaste) or can provide a service (e.g., banking). The sum of all the goods and services produced in a country is termed as GDP.

Alright. So, Why Is It Important?

Duh! It is the world's most important economic indicator.

GDP is extensively quoted in the business media and it is seen as a proxy for the overall economic health of a country. The absolute number of GDP (often reported in trillions of dollars) is seen as a measure of the size of the economy. The increase in GDP over the previous year (GDP growth rate) is often seen as a critical metric of economic growth. If you have been reading the newspapers, this term off late has been giving sleepless nights to everyone concerned.

When corporate honchos sitting in glass chambers in New York decide which country to invest their excess money in, they often look at growth in GDP as the first metric for evaluation.

The growth in GDP is often seen as a reflection of a government's ability to handle the economy. Governments carefully track GDP estimates while allocating public investments.

Hmmm... What Are the Components of GDP?

There are various approaches to come up with different components of GDP. I will not bore you with the various methods but write about the most practical one which is used on a day-to-day basis:

GDP = Private consumption + Government expenditure + Private investment + Exports – Imports.

Private consumption is the sum of goods (e.g., potato chips) and services (e.g., using a 4G service) consumed by mere mortals like you and me. Government expenditure is the amount spent by the government (e.g., infrastructure projects). This is why you hear analysts closely tracking government spending plans. Private investment refers to the investment made by private companies (e.g., company opening a new plant). Exports is what is sold (e.g., textiles) outside India while imports is what enters India (e.g., oil).

If you have been following the business press, the Indian GDP is struggling due to poor consumption growth by you and I. Consumption numbers are important as it accounts for 60 per cent of total GDP in India.[4]

How Is GDP Interpreted?

GDP estimates are released by most governments quarterly for the last few decades. The growth in GDP, expressed as a percentage, is carefully tracked. GDP growth rates come in two sizes, the nominal and real GDP. Nominal GDP implies the total output of the country factoring in inflation (read price rise) of goods. Real GDP is the more important metric that indicates the growth of an economy after removing the effects of inflation. Real GDP is proxy to actual growth that has occurred in an economy.

Once these growth percentages are released, analytics and economists jump like excited bunnies to analysing these numbers to declare which country is doing well and poorly. Then they declare with upbeat chests which is the world's fastest growing economy and so on. Two quarters of GDP decline (negative real growth) is scary and is termed as recession. A more prolonged period of declining GDP is called depression (e.g., Great Economic Depression in the United States in the 1930s).

To study historical or latest GDP estimates, the most reliable data source is provided by the World Bank or International Monetary Fund website.

Why Do I Hear 'Estimates' When Speaking about GDP? Is It Not the Actual Number?

GDP is an estimate (and a very good one) of the overall output of the country. It is not totally accurate as it doesn't capture the unorganized or the black market in totality.

While we are criticizing the metric, there is another big concern with GDP estimates. GDP is an indication of the size of the economy but doesn't account for equitable spread of growth in wealth or other social indicators. Think of a lot of countries with high GDP where the rich are becoming richer and the poor don't feel the difference. It doesn't account for average quality of living of the population.

How Does GDP for Indian Seem?

If you have been reading the newspapers, or fake news on social media, you will be aware that the Indian economy is often considered the world's fastest or second fastest growing economy. Over the last two years, its GDP growth has been hovering around 6–7.5 per cent. Off late, its growth has tapered to 4.5–5.5 per cent (pre-Covid).

Services contribute the maximum (refer to Table 3.1) to Indian GDP (52%) followed by manufacturing (31%) followed by Agriculture (17%).[5] Interestingly, agriculture provides livelihood to over 50 per cent of India's population but contributes only 17 per cent to its GDP. Meanwhile, the US economy is primarily led by services with it contributing nearly 80 per cent to its GDP.

As per the IMF (International Monetary Fund), the United States is the biggest economy (GDP of ~20 trillion $) followed by the European Union and China. India has a GDP of ~3 trillion $ and is one of the world's Top 10 economies.[6]

In conclusion, understanding GDP is one of the most pivotal concepts in business. However, GDP is rarely discussed without a detailed discussion on its nerdy sister, inflation. In the next chapter, we get a thick spectacled view into her lifestyle.

Contribution to GDP	India (%)	United States (%)
Agriculture	17	2
Manufacturing	31	20
Services	52	78
Total	100	100

Table 3.1: Contribution to Indian and American GDP by Various Sectors. Do You Notice Anything Surprising?

4

INFLATION: THE BEAST THAT ERODES MONEY

Shruti, a member of the compensation team in Human Resources, is working out the salary hikes that should be given to employees in her company. Given her company hasn't done very well, she is not sure how much to recommend. Her manager helps her out by saying, 'At least provide for inflation'.

Inflation is the mother of all economic concepts.

If there is one metric that is tracked with utmost concentration by bankers and economists the world over, it is undisputedly inflation. It is central to policy making by the government and central banks the world over. Inflation, if not managed well, can destroy economies overnight while a well-managed inflation puts a country on the path to sustainable growth.

As a concept, inflation implies the price increase in goods and services over a period of time. If a kg of potato cost ₹20 the previous year and currently costs ₹22, it has seen an inflation of 10 per cent. Inflation is always expressed as a percentage. Inflation is the reason that money loses its power over a period of time; for instance, a year earlier, ₹20 could buy 1 kg of potato but it would purchase less than a kg of potato this year.

The reason prices go up, or inflation occurs, is a simple imbalance between demand and supply of money with goods. As people earn more, more money chases a limited supply of goods and hence prices of goods go up. Inflation also occurs when companies increase prices of their products as their raw material prices have gone up. If the price of potatoes goes up, there is a likelihood that the prices of potato chips will also go up.

Inflation is measured as a basket of critical goods and services.

Inflation is calculated as a weighted average of goods and services. In India, the metric used to track inflation is termed as Consumer Price Index. The inflation index tracks increase in prices in food (milk, fruits, vegetables), fuel and power and other consumed services (recreation, transportation). In India, the Consumer Price Index, measure of inflation has been hovering in the range of 3–4 per cent over the last two to three years.[7] (For the nerds, if you are looking to understand the 100-year inflation trend in India, please visit the Notes)

A certain amount of inflation is considered healthy.

A very high inflation is harmful as it reduces the power of money. As a result, the real savings of individual households reduce dramatically. However, if inflation is lower than 0, termed as deflation, the scenario is equally gloomy. If prices keep falling, companies reduce production and liquidate inventory leading to lower employment and loss in demand. With lower employment, people spend lesser and save more leading to de-growth in the economy.

Central banks across the world target a moderate inflation in low single digits. Central banks control inflation by managing the money supply in the system. If there is too much money chasing fewer goods, they reduce the money supply by increasing interest rates so that inflation doesn't rise. If there is too little money chasing goods, they lower the interest rates so that inflation rises and reaches the target level.

Businesses look at inflation as a key metric to take pricing decisions.

Businesses track the inflation numbers very closely to decide on key business decisions. For instance, wage hikes are decided upon factoring in the expected inflation. After all, you can't pay your employees lower than last year after factoring in inflation. In addition, prices of products and services are decided after factoring in inflation. If there has been an increase in the price of a key raw material, companies look to pass on that price increase to their consumers if they can. Production amounts are decided upon after looking at inflation estimates. In case of negative inflation or deflation, companies tend to limit production as it is a larger indication of an economy with high unemployment and low desire to spend.

In summary, inflation is a key concept to understand the economy and business. It is a necessary beast that needs constant supervision. It is one of the key elements that defines pricing strategy for a product or a service. In the next chapter, we further explore this.

Is That So?

1. Did you know the inflation in Venezuela reached 450 per cent leading to total loss of value for their currency?[8]
2. Did you know Japan has experienced consistent deflation over a period of time from the 1990s?[9]

5 PRICING: WHAT'S THE FUSS ABOUT?

Pricing is an extremely critical element in any business. It is considered one of the four elements (four Ps) of the marketing mix, besides promotion, product and placement.

It is significant due to the following aspects:

- Pricing has a direct impact on consumer demand. If you charge too high in a competitive market, you lose units purchased. If you charge too low, you lose out on potential profit.
- Pricing often conveys imagery of a product. High price is often seen as a proxy for high quality (think of your pretty iPhone). A low price, although seeming fair, can destroy the product (think of how the ₹1 lakh tag destroyed the Tata Nano as it was perceived to be a cheap car).
- Pricing is a science and an art. Pricing decisions are made after studying elasticity, consumer sensitivity to change in prices. In addition, pricing has immense psychological implications. For instance, consumers perceive a huge difference in price between two identical products at ₹99 and ₹100.
- Pricing is seen as a key lever by companies to drive up profitability every year. In all budget discussions, an increase in pricing is always taken as a key business input.
- Pricing directly factors in inflation. In case inflation is increasing or decreasing, companies decide on whether pricing should be proportionally higher or lower.

Pricing strategy, for a product or service, is seen through the lens of cost, competitor, consumer and substitutes available.

Pricing is done for products (e.g., soaps, shampoo, chips) or services (e.g., Netflix, Vodafone, Utilities providers).

For a product (refer to Table 5.1), the most frequently used pricing strategies include positioning oriented, price skimming and penetrative pricing. For a service, the most frequently used pricing strategies include free + premium, subscription model and metered usage-oriented pricing. Each pricing philosophy typically factors in various inputs, namely, cost of production, competitor pricing, consumer sensitivity

Pricing For?	Pricing Philosophy	Cost	Competitor	Consumer	Substitute
Product	Positioning oriented	Yes	Yes	Yes	
	Price skimming		Yes	Yes	
	Penetrative pricing	Yes	Yes	Yes	
Service	Free + Premium		Yes	Yes	
	Subscription model		Yes	Yes	Yes
	Metered usage	Yes		Yes	
Hybrid	Product as a service	Yes	Yes	Yes	Yes

Table 5.1: Pricing Strategy, Its Associated Philosophy and Dimensions Deployed. Did You Ever Think Pricing Was So Complicated?

to price and substitute pricing. Consumer sensitivity to price is measured by elasticity of the product.

Positioning oriented pricing implies setting the price of a product basis the price of the nearest competitor. For instance, a local jeans manufacturer may decide to keep their prices 20 per cent cheaper than Levi's or Dove shampoo may price itself 10 per cent higher than Pantene. The pricing decision is a function of the brand equity the product believes it commands compared to competition. To determine the final price, elements that are considered include competitor price, consumer sensitivity to price and cost of the product in case a plan is being made to price lesser than competition.

Price skimming strategy implies setting a very high price for a new product and reducing its price over a period of time (e.g., iPhones). It is employed by companies to position a premium image and recover their costs early. The key assumption while adopting a price skimming strategy is that consumers are relatively insensitive (low elasticity) to price changes. As newer products emerge, prices of older products are lowered (think of how prices of iPhone 6 and 7 dropped with the launch of iPhone X).

Penetrative pricing strategy implies setting a very low price to capture market share and increasing prices later once a minimum threshold in sales has been reached or competition has been wiped out. For such a strategy to succeed, variable cost of manufacturing and competition pricing are the key decision points. Companies offering promotional schemes like Buy One Get One, often termed as BOGO, endorse this philosophy. The classical example of this pricing strategy has been employed by Jio, as it looked to gain market share with a very low introduction price and is now consciously increasing its prices as it has a minimum threshold of consumers.

The primary pricing strategy for service companies is often termed as 'freemium' (free + premium) pricing. This philosophy involves offering basic services for free and charging for premium services. For instance, Dropbox or iCloud or Google utilize this philosophy where a basic storage is offered free (e.g., 15 GB for Gmail) and a significantly larger size is charged to the consumer. The pricing architecture charged by Google for its photos indicates that the 100 GB plan costs you around ₹130 a month. In case 100 GB is too small for your Instagram-obsessed lifestyle, please visit their website for a complete view on the rates.

As visible, this strategy is leveraged on by technology companies. Key influencers to arrive at this decision point include competitor price and consumer willingness to pay for the service.

As the name suggests, the subscription model involves charging the consumer a fixed amount per month and a service is offered to them. Primary examples of this philosophy include Netflix or Amazon Prime. The philosophy is fairly common to magazines that charge a fixed amount and a set of content is delivered to the consumer. Key decision points to arrive at such a price involve understanding the competitor, the consumer willingness to pay and the attractiveness of the substitute (in case of Netflix, television or cable).

Metered usage is an adaptation of the freemium model where the consumer pays more as they consume more. This is one of the oldest pricing philosophies used by utilities companies (think of your electricity and water bills). Key decision points to arrive at such a price involve consumer willingness to pay and cost of production. Given that most utilities companies are monopolies, competition cost is rarely factored in.

One of the more contemporary pricing models involves converting pricing of premium products as a service. A classical example of this philosophy is the pricing of costly iPhones in the United States. Apple decided to make its phones affordable by allowing consumers to pay a monthly rent for the iPhone and the telecommunication provider rather than make them pay a high down payment at purchase.

Once pricing is agreed upon and implemented, regular review is the key to track effectiveness.

The impact of change in pricing and its resultant impact on sales volume, revenue and profit should be constantly monitored. Any adverse or unexpected change in price should be carefully deliberated upon. In addition, elasticity estimates should be regularly updated with more recent pricing changes on the ground.

In conclusion, pricing is a complex vehicle to drive business. When understood and applied well, it can leapfrog business volume and profits. If misunderstood and misapplied, it can lead to business disaster. At the end of this chapter, if you have understood the table depicted earlier (Table 5.1), you have got the pricey part of pricing.

In the next chapter, we will discuss one of the key elements of pricing, measuring and interpreting elasticity.

Food for Thought

As we come to the end of this chapter, I am writing down some of the more interesting interview questions I have asked or have come across. Take up these and see how you would approach them. There is no right answer, hence I am not prescribing a solution. However, I will provide some directional guidelines.

Apple is going to launch its next set of iPhones in September. At what price do you think should they be released in India?

Pricing is decided by a combination of cost-based pricing, substitute-based pricing, consumer willingness to pay and competition-based pricing. With Apple, as you will keep solving this question, you will realize it is only about internal benchmarking with its past models that determine its pricing. In simple English, add a certain percentage to the last year's model and you should be getting the price.

I typically give a candidate a blank sheet of paper and tell him or her it is a painting and he or she has to put a price to it. How would you approach it?

It is a pricing question. It is a function of benchmarking, with the same artist's previous work or work of similar artists. Other options include having a private auction, conducting a short survey to identify consumer willingness to pay.

6 | ELASTICITY: AM I REALLY THAT SENSITIVE?

Swati, a brand manager at a leading consumer goods company, is asked by her boss to relook at the pricing of her key product (a nutritional bar for young children). She is not sure how to approach it. (In case you have wondered why I use certain names like Mehak and Swati as examples through the book, let me clarify that they are not the names of my present girlfriends. Neither are they the names of my past girlfriends).

Pricing is one of the four key Ps of marketing besides product, promotion and placement. It is often the single biggest reason a product succeeds or fails.

As a discipline, pricing is part art and science. While the art part is left to human judgement, this chapter will address the science element in pricing. Pricing strategy involves two components, agreeing on a pricing philosophy and understanding the sensitivity of the product to a change in price. Pricing philosophy has been addressed in the previous chapter. Elasticity, or the product's sensitivity to the change in price is addressed in this chapter.

Elasticity is a measure of how sensitive your product is to a price change.

Intuitively, elasticity is a measure of how much the sales of the product reduces when the price of the product increases and vice versa. In mathematical terms, it is expressed as:

Elasticity = Change in quantity (expressed as percentage)/ Change in 1% in price

Elasticity is expressed as a ratio.

There are certain products that are highly sensitive to a change in price while some are less sensitive. Daily groceries, everyday essentials are highly sensitive to price changes while certain luxury items (e.g., your pretty iPhone, gold) rarely seem to be affected by a price change.

Elasticity	Interpretation	Examples
Less than –1 (e.g., –2, –3)	Highly elastic	Daily groceries, budget mobile phones
Between –1 and 0 (e.g., –0.5)	Moderately elastic	Apparel
Close to 0	Largely inelastic	High end gadgets (e.g., your lovely IPAD)
> 0 (e.g., +0.5, +1)	Giffen Good or inversely elastic	Expensive Rolex watches/gadgets

Table 6.1: Elasticity Intervals and Their Interpretation. Which Bucket Do You Think the BMW Series 5 Car Falls In?

Elasticity is in general a negative ratio implying as prices increase, quantities of goods sold decrease and vice versa.

Referring to Table 6.1, in case elasticity is less than –1 (e.g., –1.5, –2), it implies that the item is highly price elastic. A 1 per cent price increase will have more than a 1 per cent decrease in quantity. Items like daily groceries, budget mobile phones often belong to this category.

In case, elasticity is in the range of –1 to 0 (e.g., –0.5), it implies that the product is moderately elastic. A 1 per cent increase in price will have less than a 1 per cent decrease in quantity sold. Branded apparel often falls in this category.

In case elasticity is close to 0 (e.g., 0.1, –0.05), it implies that price and quantity of that product have little relation.

Increase in price will have negligible impact on the units of quantity sold. High-end gadgets often fall in this category.

In some extreme cases, elasticity can be higher than 1 (e.g., 1.5, 2), implying a price increase leads to an increase in sale of the product. These items are called Giffen goods and a price increase often signifies superior quality or superior brand imagery. Super premium watches like Rolex often fall in this category.

Elasticity is a function of the product's acceptability in the market.

Extent of elasticity of a product is determined by

- **Extent of brand equity:** Products with superior brand equity and consumer loyalty have lower elasticity (e.g., Gucci bags, Louis Vuitton accessories, Omega watches)
- **Availability of substitutes:** Greater the availability of substitutes, higher the elasticity and sensitivity of the product to pricing changes (e.g., unbranded rice, sugar)

Elasticity is calculated using mathematical regression.

Elasticity is calculated using statistical tools like multiple regression. The benefit of regression is that it isolates other variables that can impact sales (e.g., trade schemes, seasonality, competition behaviour) and can accurately evaluate the relationship only between changes in sales and a change in price.

A typical regression model considers 18–20 variables to model while more advanced models consider exponential regression to build it. We cover multiple regression as a later chapter in the book.

In most companies, a third-party agency often calculates elasticity for a product or a service and provides it as a six-monthly service.

Elasticity is typically used in products where prices change often and there is an ability to alter price.

Elasticity is used to evaluate price changes where the industry allows a player to alter price. In case of industries where the government (e.g., pharmaceuticals) or a market leader sets the price, elasticity has little use. Also, in industries where price changes are minimal, elasticity throws little insight into price sensitivity of the product.

In conclusion, elasticity is used to decide on pricing changes across products and services across various industries. It is often clubbed with a pricing philosophy which has been addressed in the previous chapter. Elasticity and Pricing address one of the four Ps of marketing. However, the real job a brand manager does on a day-to-day basis is slightly different. The next two chapters explore this theme.

Swati realizes that her product (a nutritional bar for young children) is highly price elastic (elasticity—1.3). Should she reduce the price blindly to sell a significantly higher number of units?

7

DOING A BRAND MANAGER'S ROLE

Mehak, managing a famous brand (Nasal Glory—a premium cream to remove overgrown nasal hair) portrayed on TV by p(r)etty damsels, is sitting in a monthly review discussion with her category lead. Her category lead asks her what exactly is going on with her brand at the ground. How does Mehak answer this question?

Why Is This Primer Relevant for You?

Being a brand manager or a marketing professional in a fast moving consumer goods (FMCG) company is a highly coveted role. Some of these roles are filled with very high-profile management graduates who have been grinding away in the heat of Northern India for many years. Irrespective of popular belief, a marketing role primarily involves understanding nuances of business through intense number crunching. And the base for most of this number crunching is a word which is synonymous with Pandora's box—the Nielsen report.

What Is the Dreaded Nielsen Report?

The Nielsen report gives details on the performance of a product/brand over a period of time. It is compiled by a market research agency titled, you guessed it, Nielsen. Nielsen collects data regularly from thousands of retailers (e.g., small grocers, large grocers, supermarkets) and builds a periodic view of the performance of the product/brand. Once this data is collected from a large sample of outlets, Nielsen extrapolates this sample to predict the performance at the universe of outlets.

What Does This Report Comprise?

Nielsen report comprises of the following cuts of data:

- Nielsen reports information at the category level (e.g., confectionary, chocolates, hair oil, shampoo) over a period of time (yearly, quarterly, etc).
- The most important metric that is reported is the market share of the product. It also reports the competitor market share and change in market share over a period of time.
- Extent of distribution (Numeric distribution): If there are five outlets as part of the universe and Nasal Glory is available in two outlets, Numeric Distribution of Nasal Glory is (2/5) 40 per cent.
- Quality of distribution (weighted distribution): The quality of distribution implies if Nasal Glory is present in the right set of outlets. It is computed as the size of the category in outlets where Nasal Glory is present

Outlet	Is Nasal Glory Present?	Value of Nasal Glory in the Outlet	Value of Category (Nasal Glory + Competition) in the Outlet
A	No	0	50
B	Yes	20	40
C	Yes	30	40
D	No	0	100
E	No	0	100

Table 7.1: Outlet-Wise Presence of Nasal Glory and the Category. Next Time You Visit Your Local *Kirana* Store, Why Don't You Try to Pester Him for All This Information and See How He Responds?

divided by the total category size across outlets (please refer to Table 7.1).

WD = Category size of outlets where Nasal Glory is present (40 [Outlet B] + 40 [Outlet C])/
Category size of all outlets (50 + 40 + 40 + 100 + 100)
WD = 24 per cent.

The weighted distribution (24%) is more important than the numeric distribution (40%) as it is important to be present in the larger outlets rather than the smaller outlets.

- Share of counter where Nasal Glory is present (Share among handlers): It indicates the share of Nasal Glory compared to all the brands in that category present in the outlets.
- Other metrics like total stock, value of sales from each outlet and stock turnover ratio are also reported. These are often considered for advanced analysis.

How Do You Make Sense of This Report?

The Nielsen reports helps in analysing the driver for change in market share (refer to Figure 7.1):

- Is the change happening because the product was available in lesser number of outlets? (Numeric distribution).
- Is the change happening because the product was not available in larger outlets? (Weighted distribution).
- Is the change happening because the product is available at the store but is not selling as fast as the competitor product at the shelf? (Counter share or share amount handlers).
- Let me assist you some benchmarks. A brand that leads in a market will typically have 65–75 per cent numeric distribution and a weighted distribution in

excess of 90 per cent. In case this reads like Hebrew, just ignore it.

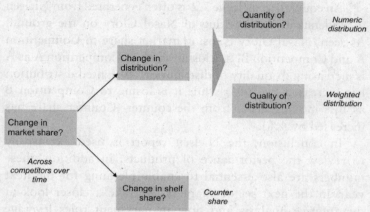

Figure 7.1: Reasons for Change in Market Share. Can You Come Up with Another

Product	Market Share (%)/Change from Previous Period (%)	Numeric Distribution (%)/Change from Previous Period (%)	Weighted Distribution (%)/Change from Previous Period (%)	Counter Share (%)/Change from Previous Period (%)
Nasal Glory	12% (change –2%)	45% (change 1%)	54% (change –2%)	17% (change –1%)
Competition A	8% (change +1%)	35% (change 0%)	60% (change 10%)	11% (change 0%)
Competition B	7% (change +1%)	30% (change 0%)	38% (change 1%)	13% (change 4%)

Table 7.2: Change in Market Share, Numeric Distribution, Weighted Distribution and Counter Share for Nasal Glory and Its Nosy Competitors

Reason?

An equivalent of Table 7.2 is often generated from Nielsen to understand the working of Nasal Glory on the ground. As seen, Nasal Glory is losing market share to Competition A and Competition B. It is losing share to Competition A as A is increasing its quality of distribution (Weighted distribution has increased by 10%) while it is losing to Competition B as B is moving faster from the counter (Counter share has increased by 4%).

In conclusion, the Nielsen report is used extensively to review the performance of products. In addition, these numbers are also essential to enable planning for the next year. In the next set of chapters, we take a closer look at quantitative analysis and how management roles leverage data to drive business decisions.

8 BORING BUT NECESSARY NUMBERS: PART I

Operating in a business environment is often about understanding key business metrics. While reporting of business metrics is fairly common, interpretation of these numbers is the key for any business decision maker. As part of this chapter, we look at primary ways to analyse data in a business environment.

Movie	Business (₹ Cr)
Bharat	197
Race 3	166
Tiger Zinda Hai	339
Tubelight	114
Sultan	300
Prem Ratan Dhan Payo	194
Bajrangi Bhaijaan	315
Kick	211
Jai Ho	109
Dabangg 2	149
Ek Tha Tiger	186
Bodyguard	144
Ready	120
Dabangg	141

(continued)

(continued)

Movie	Business (₹ Cr)
Veer	38
London Dreams	25
Main aurr Mrs Khanna	7.3
Wanted	60

Table 8.1: Business Realized of the Past Few Movies of Bollywood Superstar, Salman Khan. Did You Think His Movies Do More Business in General or Less?

Source: Here is the detailed link to the collections of *Bhai's* movies—https://www.businesstoday.in/trending/box-office/dabangg-3-box-office-collection-salman-khan-film-enters-the-coveted-rs-200-crore-club/story/393222.html

For the purpose of discussion, we will consider the revenues of the last few movies of Bollywood superstar, Salman Khan. My apologies in case you don't like Salman Khan, you are free to use a movie star of your choice in Table 8.1.

The key question often is, how have his movies been doing? Let us take a deeper look.

On Average, How Much Do His Movies Generate?

The simplest measure to understand how his movies have been performing is to calculate the mean or a simple average. The mean is computed by a function 'average' in Microsoft Excel. In this case, the average revenue Salman Khan's movies have garnered is ₹156 crores. To understand if this number is good or bad, this average is compared to other movie actors to see relative performance. Any guesses on how much Shah Rukh Khan's movies are garnering? Quick hint: It is significantly lower.

In business, the mean is often employed to understand average return by a company stock, average profit after tax and so on. However, the criticism with this metric is that it gets influenced by outliers, for instance revenues that are too low (e.g., *Main aurr Mrs Khanna* generated a revenue of ₹7.3 Crores) or too high (e.g., *Tiger Zinda Hai* generated a revenue of ₹339 Crores) compared to the mean.

Hence, we also look at the median to get an understanding of averages.

The median is used to overcome the problem of outliers. Statistically, it is the middle number in a series of data points arranged in an ascending or descending order. In case there are an odd number of data points, the median is the middle number—(n + 1)/2 data point. In case there are an even number of observations, the median is the middle number computed by the average of the n/2 and (n + 1)/2 data points. In this case, the median business generated by Salman Khan's movies is 146. 5 Crores which is the average of *Bodyguard* (₹144 Crores) and *Dabangg 2* (₹149 Crores).

In business, it is also applied to scenarios to build an understanding of average return of a large number of investments, average profits across a portfolio of companies after factoring in outliers.

Do Salman Khan's Movies Generate a Wide Range of Business Away from the Average?—(Part I)

In addition to understanding the mean or the median, it is important to understand the internal spread of data points. Do the data points tend to cluster around the average or do they tend to cluster away from the mean? This is answered by the metric called standard deviation. It is calculated as:

Standard deviation = Square root of ([Summation of (Data point – Average)²]/(n – 1)}.

You can ignore the above formula if you find it resembling Hebrew. It is interpreted as follows, ~70 per cent of the data points fall within average plus or minus one standard deviation. In our example, movies of Salman Khan operate with a standard deviation of ₹95 Crores. This translates to the interpretation that 70 per cent of his movies range between 61 Crores (Average (156) – Standard deviation (95)) and 252 Crores (Average (156) + Standard deviation (95)). As you can see, it is a fairly wide range.

Do Salman Khan's Movies Generate a Wide Range of Business Away from the Average?—(Part 2)

Mathematically, the internal spread of data points is also evaluated using a metric termed as coefficient of variation. It is calculated as:

Coefficient of variation = Standard deviation/Mean.

In our case, the coefficient of variation is 95/156 translating to 61 per cent. Any coefficient of variation above 30 per cent indicates a high internal clustering away from the mean. In this case, Salman Khan's movies tend to have a high internal clustering away from his average of ₹156 Crores as it is 30 per cent on either side of the mean.

Both these functions can be calculated in Microsoft Excel. Standard deviation is calculated using STDEV function and coefficient of variation can be calculated as standard deviation divided by the mean. These functions are often deployed in business to understand inherent volatility in return across a portfolio of investments.

In conclusion, there are numerous methods to understanding business metrics. While there are many more metrics, these four collection of metrics (mean, median, standard deviation and coefficient of variation) are an excellent starting point to understanding business metrics. I would strongly advise you to practise these four functions in Microsoft Excel on a data set of your choice. The exercise will hold you in very good stead.

In the next chapter, we look at simple techniques to make sense of hardcore business data.

9

BORING BUT NECESSARY NUMBERS: PART 2

Mehak receives a large dump of data on a Monday morning about a company's performance. Her supervisor asks her to do a rough analysis to come up with preliminary trends.

Data analysis is equivalent to a giant black box that encompasses everything in its radar. From the ordinary to the majestic, this field of study has an incredible level of complexity potentially requiring years to master. However, like most things in life, there is a simple cheat sheet or quick fix that can help in providing a great starting point. As the chapter demonstrates, the following cuts of data are the most important to start with to understand company or business unit performance. We looked at Data Analysis 101 comprising of mean, median, standard deviation and coefficient of variation in the previous chapter. We look at Data Analysis 102 in this primer.

External Benchmarking: How Is the Company Faring with respect to the Market?

The best starting point is to evaluate the performance of the company with respect to the market. Prima facie views on change in the market share of the company is an excellent starting point.

As can be seen from Table 9.1, the two largest players, ABC (the company under study) and its lead competitor have lost market share (change in ABC's market share is –2%) to the unorganized players (they have gained 3% and 1% in market share). Prima facie, it indicates a broad trend of unorganized

Company	Market Share 2017 (%)	Market Share 2018 (%)	Change in Market Share (%)
ABC (company under study)	23	21	–2%
Lead competitor 1	16	15	–1%
Unorganized local player 1	8	11	3%
Unorganized local player 2	6	7	1%
Others	47	46	–1%

Table 9.1: Change in Market Share Numbers for ABC and Its Competition. In the Real World, if ABC Ever Lost Market Share Like This, You Would Be Jumping Like a Cat on a Hot Tin Roof

players becoming more competitive. If more data is available, the same analysis can be done at greater granular levels (e.g., product category). In most cases, more granular industry data is unavailable.

Internal Benchmarking: How Are Things Shaping Up Internally?

To benchmark performance using internal data, it is sliced along three entities—product, region and customer. Furthermore, each of these entities are analysed along two dimensions, salience (expressed as percentage of total) and historical growth rate. This view across three entities along two dimensions often presents the best view to start internal benchmarking.

As can be seen from Table 9.2, although product lines 2 and 3 are growing in high single digits, the overall growth rate

Product	Revenue 2017 (₹ Crore)	Salience (%)	Growth Rate (%)
Product Line 1	100	76	5
Product Line 2	20	15	9
Product Line 3	10	7	10
Total	130	100	6

Table 9.2: Revenue, Contribution to Total Sales (salience) and Growth Rate for the Various Product Lines. It Doesn't Take a Mathematical Genius to Figure Out What Is Going on Here, Does It?

is 6 per cent because their main product line with a salience of 76 per cent is growing at 5 per cent.

In conclusion, basic external benchmarking by assessing trends in market share and internal benchmarking by assessing trends in salience and historical growth are great starting points to evaluate company performance. These are combined with mean, median, standard deviation and coefficient of variation to give a very good understanding of what is happening in the market.

In the next chapter, we look at the holy grail of mathematics for business leaders, the concept of multiple regression.

10

CAN YOU MATHEMATICALLY ANSWER WHY I AM PUTTING ON WEIGHT?

Before I get into the live example, I highly recommend you not to have this mathematical conversation with your girlfriend, fiancé or your spouse on why she is putting on weight. The consequences of such a conversation might turn out to be very ugly.

May the Force Be with You

Do you want to predict how much company sales will be if I increase marketing spend by 1 per cent or increase pricing by 1 per cent or if Diwali is expected to be a blockbuster season this year? Enter Prince Charming below.

One of the most powerful concepts in business is to understand the methodology of regression. It explores the relationship between multiple variables. For instance, a regression model can predict the outcome in the form of a company's revenues and its relation with input variables, namely, industry growth, marketing spends, seasonality, pricing and so on. The variable that is being predicted is termed as the dependent variable (e.g., company sales) and the list of variables (e.g., marketing spend, industry growth, pricing) that are being used to predict are called independent variables. Mathematically it is defined as:

$Y = A + B1X1 + B2X2 + B3X3 + so\ on.$
$Y = Dependent\ variable\ (e.g.,\ company\ sales)$

A = Termed as slope or fixed coefficient
X1 to X3 = Independent variables (e.g., marketing spend, pricing, industry growth)
B1 to B3 = Coefficients of the independent variables.

The regression model is a mathematical equation, the quality of the mathematical model is defined by the metric R square and the importance of each independent variable is defined by its p value and coefficient.

The strength of the regression model, implying how well the mathematical equation explains the actual historical values is termed as R square. This is important as the historical correlation among the variables is used to predict the future relations.

It is also termed as quality of regression fit. An R square (R^2) of greater than 70 per cent implies that the mathematical regression model is able to explain 70 per cent of the historical data relationships between the variables accurately. For a regression model to be taken seriously, the R^2 cut off is generally taken at 75 per cent.

To evaluate if each independent variable (e.g., marketing spend, industry growth, pricing) is important or not, we use the statistical measure termed as 'p-value'. If the p-value is less than 0.05, the independent variable (e.g., marketing spend, industry growth, pricing) is significant in its relationship with the dependent variable (e.g., company sales). In layman language, this variable matters if you have to evaluate company sales.

The extent of relationship is indicated by its coefficient—the terms B1 to B3 in the above equations.

For instance, if the regression model turns out to be the following:

Sales = 7 + 1.2 × Industry growth + 2.5 × Marketing spends + 0.05 × Pricing.

If the R square is above 75 per cent, then we say that the model is good as it can explain 75 per cent of the historical associations between sales and independent variables like industry growth, marketing spends and pricing. Hence, this model can be used to predict the future sales.

If the p-value of industry growth is 0.03 (<0.05), it has a significant role in determining company sales. If the p value of marketing spends is 0.25 (>0.05), it is not significant enough to explain company sales. If the p-value of pricing is 0.02 (<0.05), it is significant to explain the relation with company sales. To evaluate future sales, marketing spends as a variable should be ignored in the formula while industry growth and pricing should be considered in the mathematical formula.

The importance of the independent variables (e.g., industry growth, pricing) in explaining the dependent variable (e.g., company sales) is determined by their coefficients. In this case, the coefficient of industry growth is 1.2 while the coefficient of pricing is 0.05. As the coefficient of industry growth is higher than the coefficient of pricing, it will have a greater role in explaining company sales.

All these statistical measures can be easily calculated in Microsoft Excel.

Multiple regression can be performed easily in Microsoft Excel. In the 'Data' tab, click on Analysis and select Regression. Indicate the dependent variable as Y (e.g., sales) and the independent variables as X (e.g., industry growth) and the confidence level at 95. The operation will throw you the R square (quality of fit) along with the p values of each independent variable (is the variable significant) and the coefficients of those variables (how sensitive are they in impacting the dependent variable).

Regression has a critical importance in business forecasting, optimization and understanding ground reality.

Regression has many applications in business. It can be used in forecasting future sales basis past patterns. It can

CAN YOU MATHEMATICALLY ANSWER WHY I AM PUTTING ON WEIGHT?

45

be used to predict mutual fund returns basis a set of independent variables.

It can be used to optimize spends and reduce spends on variables that are not significant in impacting the dependent variable. For instance, if the regression model predicts that in-store advertising is not working to drive company sales but celebrity endorsements are working very well to drive company sales, then a portion of funds can be shifted from in-store advertising to celebrity endorsements.

In fact, regression can be used by a movie house to predict how a superstar's future movies will do at the box office too. Some of the independent variables for this include timing of release (e.g., Diwali), what other movies are releasing together, general behaviour of the economy, presence of an item song, length of the movie and so on.

Regression is different from simple correlation and it is important to understand the difference.

A correlation between two variables is an indication of joint movement, for instance there is a correlation between rainfall and price of wheat. However, it is different from regression that it doesn't indicate which is the independent and the dependent variable. For instance, in our example, correlation will not indicate if sales is driven by pricing or is pricing driven by sales. In addition, correlation between two variables might not be related. For instance, there might be a correlation between the waistlines of mice and the number of centuries Virat Kohli hits but there is no underneath relation.

11

IS THIS INDUSTRY ATTRACTIVE?

Jyoti, a management graduate, is asked by her private equity client to evaluate the attractiveness of the social media industry. She has been asked to answer the following question in simple English, 'Should we enter the social media business or not?'

One of the most elementary concepts taught in business schools is Porter's Five Forces, an introduction to evaluation of attractiveness of an industry. Developed by Michael Porter[10] in the late 1970s, it has been a pivotal concept despite the criticisms associated with it. The key construct of this framework is that it evaluates the attractiveness of an industry as a whole and not for a player in that industry.

As the name suggests, industry attractiveness is a function of five key forces.

As per the framework (refer to Figure 11.1), there are five key forces that determine industry attractiveness—bargaining power of consumers, bargaining power of suppliers, threat of substitutes, threat of new entrants and industry rivalry. This section will leverage this framework using the social media industry (e.g., Facebook, LinkedIn, Instagram, Twitter) as an illustrative industry.

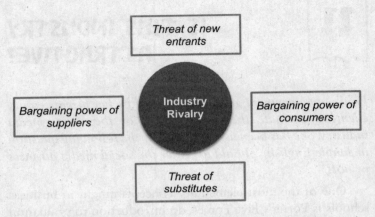

Figure 11.1: The Porter's 5 Forces Framework. Do You Think It Is Intuitively Right? Can You Look to Improve on It?

Industry attractiveness is higher when bargaining power of consumers is lower or limited.

When there are a large number of consumers, bargaining power of consumers is lower than when the end consumer is a handful of B2B (business-to-business) clients. Bargaining power of consumers is a function of their switching costs, price sensitivity and availability of substitutes. In case of government sanctioned infrastructure projects, the bargaining power of the end consumer, the government, is much higher than the bargaining power of consumers in a healthcare industry where only two to three companies produce a critical drug. In our example of social media, bargaining power of consumers is relatively low as there are only a few successful platform providers like Facebook, Google, LinkedIn, Instagram and switching cost of photographs, videos and network of friends from one platform to another can seem disproportionately high.

Industry attractiveness is higher when there are a lower number of available substitutes.

A substitute is an element the end consumer can choose to undertake instead of consuming your product or service. For cable TV, Netflix or YouTube is a substitute while healthy fruit drinks can be a substitute to Coca Cola. In most B2C (business-to-consumer) or consumer-oriented industries operating today, threat of substitutes is high. In case of social media, the available substitutes for the end consumer can imply a myriad of options including playing outside, meeting friends over coffee, reading a book, relaxing or sleeping at home. The biggest substitute to whiling away time on social media can be to read this book.

Industry attractiveness is higher when the bargaining power of suppliers is lower.

When there are a large number of suppliers and their ability to negotiate is lower, industry attractiveness is higher. For instance, for an FMCG company which procures from individual farmers, the bargaining power of suppliers, farmers in this case, is lower. However, in case of suppliers supplying critical equipment, for instance engines being supplied to passenger aircrafts, their buying power is relatively higher. In case of social media, the suppliers include content providers who are individual consumers themselves. Their supplier power is moderate as they cannot bargain collectively with the platform provider (e.g., Facebook, LinkedIn) but they can easily shift their content to another equally established provider.

Industry attractiveness is higher when the threat of new entrants is lower.

When it is easy to enter a new industry, the threat to existing players of an industry becomes larger. Barriers to entry for a

new player may include capital required to set-up a manufacturing plant (an industrial product), patents necessary to
operate (pharmaceutical drugs) or government policy (a commercial bank). In case of social media, the biggest barrier to
entry is the lack of network effect for the new entrant. In
case of social media, there are one to two established players
only that can provide the network—Facebook and Instagram
in case of recreation and LinkedIn in case of professional
context—to end consumers. For a new player to build millions of connections overnight can be very difficult.

*Industry attractiveness is higher when there is a lower degree
of competitive intensity.*

When there is a lot of internal competition (e.g., telecommunication in India), the ability to charge a price premium
reduces and hence the industry attractiveness goes down. The
competitiveness in an industry is a function of differentiation
that can be attained by the individual players pursuing the
routes of differentiation in features, service quality or brand.
In case of social media, internal competition is between a few
sets of ecosystem players, Facebook which owns Instagram
and WhatsApp, LinkedIn, Twitter and Google. As a result,
the internal competition is moderate.

*The five forces of porter have been met with more than five
sets of criticisms.*

While this framework has always been seen as a great starting
point, its relevance in contemporary business is increasingly
being questioned. In contemporary businesses, an entity plays
multiple roles, for instance Amazon can be your supplier,
consumer and the platform provider at the same time. In
case of social media, consumers are suppliers and consumers
of content on the same forum. In addition, it is difficult to
define clear industries for technology companies. Google may
be classified as a technology company, an advertising agency,

a travel portal, an insurance provider and so on. The single biggest criticism of Porter's five forces is that all five forces are considered equal.

Despite all these criticisms, the lens of Porter's five forces is a great starting point to structure an individual's thoughts for further analysis.

After the preliminary analysis based on Porter's five forces, Jyoti arrives at the opinion that at an aggregate level, the attractiveness of social media seems low because of the requirement of network effect (low threat of new entrants) and established well-entrenched players (moderate internal competition). She then heads back to checking her feed on Instagram.

12 LEVERAGED BUYOUT: THE EDUCATED GAMBLER!

Borrow money to buy a company, then turn that company around and rake in the moolah!

Leveraged buyout (LBO), or as the term indicates, implies the use of debt, also termed as leverage, to buy another company. The primary driver of this purchase is when the acquirer believes the target company is significantly undervalued. Hence, by using outside capital, the acquirer tries to buy out his target. The acquirer needs to borrow outside capital as the target entity might be massive and he or she might not have adequate funds of her own. In addition, if the target is doing relatively alright, the cost of borrowing money is lesser than the return on equity of the target company, hence amplifying the return. For instance, if the cost of borrowing money is 2 per cent and the target entity is generating a return on equity (return on its existing business) of 10 per cent, there is a potential upside by acquiring that company.

Isn't It a Massive Risk to Borrow Billions for a Distant Potential Opportunity?

To start on a positive note, the move can be profitable if the target entity is profitable and undervalued. In some cases, the management of the target ends up buying out the company if it believes its stock is significantly undervalued. This process is also called a management buyout. An LBO can also be considered to create a stronger joint entity if the acquirer believes that there are common synergies (high society term for common costs that can be reduced if the acquisition happens). In some cases, the acquiring firm might believe they can run the company better and make more money in the process. There are companies, also termed as private equity firms in contemporary parlance, which are in the business of buying a good target at a low price, running the business efficiently and selling it to the public or other owners making a disproportionate benefit.

Needless to say, the move is fraught with risk. Acquiring such a target with borrowed money can easily go wrong. If the move isn't right and if the target flounders, the cost of debt might burden the company debilitating its finances. If the acquisition process isn't smooth and the target starts floundering, the interest cost on the debt can lead the acquirer to the path of bankruptcy. As history proves it, there are more cases of LBOs going wrong than right.

So, Where Is the Moolah?

There are three ways to go broke—liquor, ladies and leverage. Now the truth is the first two have been added because they also start with the letter L. It is only leverage!

Warren Buffett, the greatest investor of our times, has been a harsh critic of LBOs. He has held complete disdain for the LBO crowd, or termed as the 'Private Equity' crowd in contemporary parlance. His disdain originates from their methodology of driving debt (seen as bad) up a target's financial statements and reducing equity (seen as a good thing). In addition, an LBO buy out often leads to job loss, reduction in founder control and mindless selling and buying of a target firm. He often cites the brutal acquisition of RJR Nabisco, a tobacco and food company, by Kohlberg Kravis Roberts. The deal valued at $25 bn, one of the largest ever made, was ground-breaking for the brutality shown while acquiring it and the relentless buyouts of other companies that followed. However, RJR Nabisco ended up being broken in a few years. After 15 years, KKR booked a loss on RJR Nabisco bringing to end the poster boy story of the LBO world.[11]

However, there have been strong successes to the LBO or the private equity (PE) story. One of the biggest has been the buyout of Hilton Hotels by the Blackstone Group for $26 bn in 2007.[12] Although the deal suffered initial setbacks, the deal became the most profitable private equity deal ever made when the company went public in 2013. The investors made an estimated $12 billion. In 2013, Dell decided to buy out all its public shares and go private. It is considered a very successful move with a return of investment of over 10 per cent.

Other famous deals include Toys R Us, Hertz Corporation and Metro Goldwyn Mayer.

In India, the PE industry has been on the upswing. In 2017 alone, they made a total investment of $24 bn with investments in Fortis Healthcare, Vishal Mega Mart and Star Health. Needless to say, the regular investments in technology unicorns like Flipkart, Ola Cabs and Paytm have been driven by the private equity industry.

In conclusion, the private equity industry is a high risk, high return game which is certainly not for the fainthearted.

Is That So?

1. Did you know that with an LBO, the existing creditors of the target firm become the big losers, as they are now owed money by a firm with much larger debt?
2. Did you know that Mitt Romney, the US Presidential candidate in the 2016 elections, used to lead private equity major Bain Capital?
3. Did you know that Toys R Us, bought as part of an LBO, filed for bankruptcy in late 2017?

4. Did you know that 80 per cent of LBOs happened after 2007 in emerging markets like India, China, Russia and Brazil?
5. Did you know that detergent manufacturer Nirma acquired Lafarge assets in 2016 for ₹9,300 Crores?

GROWTH STRATEGY; SELLING A DREAM

A strategy team at a large Indian conglomerate, comprising of MBA graduates, is looking to develop a 5-year-growth strategy for their parent company. They are looking for a good starting point to structure and guide their thought process.[13]

Given the volatile economic environment over the last few quarters, the single biggest agenda in most corporate boardrooms is to drive revenue growth. While everybody thinks and realizes that drawing up a growth strategy is important, in reality it is a little tricky to complete this exercise. Such an exercise needs to be structured and exhaustive comprising of quantitative and qualitative inputs. This chapter looks at a starting template of the list of questions to be answered to accomplish this exercise.

In case you are wondering why this is important for you, you will be asking yourself every day in your corporate life, how do I grow my company, my business or my own self?

Are You Playing in the Right Game?

Any growth strategy exercise begins in understanding the details of the industry the incumbent is operating in. There are many frameworks to support in this exercise with Porter's five forces being the most common starting point. Following questions are essential:

- What is the size of the industry?
- What are the key growth drivers/expected growth rate of the industry?
- Who are the key competitors and what is their competitive intensity?

- What is the expected impact of regulation and government legislation?
- What is the magnitude of digital disruption the industry is exposed to?
- What are the other related industries (that use similar raw material or distribution chains) that can be explored?

Where to Play?

Once the game (aka industry) has been identified, it is important to understand the positions the players (aka focus pockets of growth) will occupy. Following questions will help answer the main question on where to play:

- Which channels should be focused on due to existing size and future growth potential?
- Which regions should be focused on due to existing size and future growth potential?
- Which product should be focused on due to existing size and future growth potential?
- Which customer segments should be focused on due to existing size and future growth potential?
- Which price points should be focused on due to existing size and future growth potential?

Golden Question—Build, Borrow or Buy?

The most important question is often the mode of growth that the incumbent should pursue. INSEAD professor Laurence Capron in her book *Build, Borrow or Buy*[14] has identified determining mode of growth as a major driver of success in devising a growth strategy. Deciding on the mode of growth is a function of the following questions:

- What is the level of control the incumbent wants to keep on the growth strategy initiatives?
- Does the incumbent have the in-house capability to execute the growth strategy initiatives?
- What is the level of financial investment the incumbent is ready to make to pursue growth?

'Build' or growing in-house capability is pursued when the incumbent has the capability internally. It is generally used to build a greater reach for an existing product in an existing segment. It involves complete control of the execution.

'Borrow' or growing via partnerships (e.g., contracting, outsourcing) is pursued when the incumbent has a clearly defined scope or outcome statement without the threat of the partner becoming a potential competitor. It is typically used for leveraging an existing product for distribution in a new market. In such a set-up, control is shared while financial investment is not very high.

'Buy' or pursuing the inorganic route, often touted as the most risky alternative, is seen as a last resort to drive growth. It is often used to build market share or enter a completely new set-up. Control and scale are seen as primary drivers while these marriages often end up in divorce (e.g., failure rates of mergers and acquisitions (M&As) are often higher than 50%). The financial investment in such a proposition is often the largest among the various routes.

In terms of strategy, a combination of 'build and borrow' is often tried first and 'buy' is seen as a mode of last resort.

Are You Planning to Pursue Mindless Growth

Numerous companies, new age and traditional, are falling prey to the trap of pursuing mindless growth at the cost of sacrificing eventual profits. While growth leads to scale which can lead to profitability, an expansion strategy that compromises on profits is never advisable. Following questions should be carefully answered:

- Is the return on capital employed from growth initiatives higher than the cost of capital?
- Is the cost of acquisition and servicing equal to the potential lifetime profit from the consumer? In other words, will serving a particular customer ever make money for you?
- What are the key financials (Net Present Value) of the incremental initiatives over 3, 5 and 10 years?

In conclusion, growth is the magical potion being hunted for in most corporate boardrooms. The exercise to devise a growth strategy needs to be thorough and structured. And sometimes, it is okay to continue status quo rather than pursue value destroying growth activities.

Is That So?

1. Did you know that devising a growth strategy exercise typically takes between 2 and 4 months?
2. Did you know that most business conglomerates refresh their growth strategies every year as part of their annual planning exercise?
3. Did you know that according to a recent Harvard Business Review report, the failure report for M&A sits between 70 and 90 per cent?

14 | GAME THEORY: SELFISH OR CO-OPERATE?

In the movie A Beautiful Mind, *John Nash, played by Russell Crowe, is in a bar with four of his friends when a beautiful blonde and four of her friends walk in. They begin to discuss economic theories to further their strategies to get close to the ladies. They quote Adam Smith who suggests that each person should attempt to maximize their self-interest and as a result, all of them should attempt to woo the beautiful blonde. John Nash argues it is optimal for them to work for everyone's benefit and they should woo the four ladies accompanying the beautiful blonde. That configuration will lead to maximum benefit for everyone. That, in a summary, is game theory.*

Game theory is the science of strategy in social situations.

As the above scenario in the bar shows, game theory is the science of strategy in handling social situations especially when one player's action is contingent on the strategy chosen by the other player. Prominent personalities in this area of study include John von Neumann and the legendary John Nash. It has its applications in trade negotiations, market entry strategy decisions, union labour negotiations among many everyday business situations. In market entry situations, when a new player decides to enter a market, the reaction by the incumbent and the new player to each other is an apt illustrative of this theory. If both decide to brutally compete on price, both bleed. If both decide to compete on value, everybody wins. Table 14.1 illustrates the principle.

When A and B charge ₹40 each, both make a profit of ₹30. At this price, each firm has the incentive to drop its price to ₹20 and make a profit of ₹35. If both end up doing this, both end up with zero profit. The ideal stable system is when both charge ₹40 and make a profit of ₹30 each. In the real world, this strategy is often employed between service providers (e.g., telecom, cable, financial services) as they don't actively slash prices but keep focussing on providing

Option of Price Charged By Each Firm and the Resulting Profit Made By Each of Them		Price Charged by Business B (₹/unit)	
		40	20
Price charged by Business A (₹/unit)	40	30 A, 30 B	–5 A, 35 B
	20	35 A, –5 B	0 A, 0 B

Table 14.1: Prices Charged By Each Firm and Resultant Profit Made By Each of Them

Option of Mike and His Associate Confessing and the Resulting Punishment		Action Taken by his Associate	
		Confess	Deny
Action taken by Mike Ross	Confess	Both get 5 years	Mike:1 year, Associate: 10 years
	Deny	Mike: 10 years, Associate: 1 year	Both escape

Table 14.2: Option of Mike Ross and His Associate Choosing Their Actions and Resultant Penalty. Did Mike Confess? Unlikely, He Is Very Smart. Did the Cops Get His Associate to Confess?

Source: Hit TV series *Suits*.

greater value.

The Prisoner's dilemma is the most well-illustrated example of game theory. It is best represented through a scene enacted out from the hit sitcom *Suits* where Mike Ross and his associate are being interrogated by the police in different cells.

In the above scenario (refer to Table 14.2), both Mike Ross and his associate begin by denying their involvement in an insider crime. The investigators try and make them confess by playing one against the other. They keep telling each of them that if the other guy confesses and you don't, you will get 10 years. In the end, both choose not to confess and escape.

In conclusion, game theory bases itself on each person being rational and realistic. However, as behavioural economics has shown, rationality is left wanting at times by human behaviour. In addition, it is a theory that is applicable when there are a few dominant players. In modern-day business, it is a scenario not seen very often.

With most digital businesses striving for a 'winner takes all' model, best illustrated by Facebook, Google and Amazon, choosing a scenario where everybody wins might be suboptimal.

In the next chapter, we explore the dimension that is exactly the opposite of the left brain-oriented game theory advocate, the right brain-oriented behavioural psychology.

15

VAGARIES OF THE HUMAN MIND

Mehak, an experienced MBA from a leading business school, walks into a discussion with a large vendor. Her vendor asks for a ridiculous commission to do business with her company.[15]

Although she is well trained to handle such situations, how can she effectively bargain while maximizing value for her company?

Most conventional education systems lay primary emphasis on left brain-dominated analytical intelligence. Good business transactions are often seen as a product of sound analytical rigour, numerical intelligence, fact-based negotiation and so on. In reality, however, it is the non-analytical brain that dominates interactions, professional and personal, among individuals. The human mind, no matter how rational, is also equipped to cloud its rational side with a list of thinking errors often referred to as Cognitive Biases. The chapter looks at some of the more common situations involving these biases we encounter on a day-to-day basis. *(There are numerous books that capture the vagaries of the human mind with great ease while making it a highly engaging read—*Nudge, Misbehaving *and* Thinking Fast and Slow. *I would strongly urge you to buy and read all the three books but only after you have bought all of my books).*

I will keep referring to Mehak as the protagonist in all the anecdotes. And that is not a bias.

Mehak is trying to research on the potential of portable steel toilets in India. She is trying to go through archives of news articles. Implicitly, she tends to open those that favour her initial thought of the segment being highly attractive.

The 'Confirmation Bias' is the tendency to look for evidence that supports an inbuilt theory and implicitly reject or discount evidence that disproves it. The best way to overcome this bias is to always run all evidence past another person or someone completely outside that sphere of work.

Mehak walks into a client meeting as an external consultant and gives a presentation on the future of the portable steel toilets in India. She looks professional, well-groomed and impressive, sounds crisp, diligent and thorough. The audience is impressed.

The audience, initially unaware of the segment and largely unaware after the presentation, gives her a thumbs up. Classical case of the 'Halo Effect'. The 'Halo Effect' bias is the tendency of an audience to favour a person basis the supposition of a halo, manifested through an impressive personality. It is difficult to get rid of this bias consciously, but the best way is to avoid taking any decision quickly and waiting patiently to absorb the real picture over a period of time.

After Mehak's impressive presentation, over lunch, one of the client members asks Mehak on the number one issue affecting India. Mehak refers to the growing anguish of a social media enthusiast. They all nod in unison.

The 'Availability Bias' implies subjects that tend to believe what the world has become basis the stories that are primarily available. Outrageous media coverage of seemingly less important issues can become deal breakers to forming realistic opinions. It is very difficult to overcome this bias unless there is a conscious attempt to stay detached from day-to-day affairs.

This is one of the reasons why most TV channels seem to cover stories that don't seem to matter to the silent majority. A classical case of 'Availability Bias'.

Mehak is called for a second presentation to detail out some of her hypothesis. She is equally well prepared, but the impact is not as good as the first one. Some of the client members begin to ask her really tough questions.

There are multiple biases that are at play here. The 'Law of Small Numbers' refers to the fact that most things tend to average over time. One good day will eventually be followed up with a below average day. The 'Halo Bias', also at play here, over the period of time, tends to subside once people start entering details in the fine print.

As Mehak realizes that the presentation is getting tricky, she decides to avoid number heavy slides and resorts to narrating a story. A story of a widowed woman in rural India whose only way out of poverty is to look at portable steel toilets. The audience begins to get a 'real-life pulse' of the potential of the product.

'Representativeness', or the tendency to predict the universal from the specific, is a double-edged sword. If largely true, it is an excellent tool to get people to appreciate the underlying drivers in any study. However, a good story can hide the flaw that the universal may not be inferred from the specific. The easiest way to counter a good story is to come up with another story that proves the absolute opposite.

After the meeting, Mehak steps outside the building for a quick smoke. Her client counterparts, smoking a few feet away, start shuddering in disbelief. They decide to reconsider if she is the right person they want to work with.

'Stereotyping Bias' refers to an expectation of behaviour from a certain person depending on factors like gender, race, age, affluence without factoring in the individual identity. It can be tricky as a stereotype often has negative connotations with some of them being linked to poorer performance, immoral behaviour or lack of professionalism.

Another bias that comes along with 'Stereotyping Bias' is 'Hindsight Bias' and 'Overconfidence Bias'. If you have ever noticed your boss say *'I told you so'* or *'I am 100 per cent* sure what I am saying is correct', you should infer the bias he or she is suffering from. It is best to walk out of such conversations as they are rarely constructive.

In conclusion, cognitive biases play a critical role in our interactions with others. While some of them are genetic, some of them have been implicitly absorbed from our environment or developed from personal experiences. While it is difficult to train the mind to overcome years of 'nature and nurture' grooming, a few quick fixes will do no harm.

Finally, Mehak should probably read Thinking, Fast and Slow *by Daniel Kahneman. He would refer to the scenario mentioned at the beginning of the chapter as a typical case of the 'Anchoring Effect'. The 'Anchoring Effect' is the tendency to ensure the first number thrown is the benchmark for further negotiations. As Daniel would advise, Mehak should avoid the trap of the 'Anchoring Effect' with her vendor and walk out of the negotiation.*

16

UNDERSTANDING THE NET WORKING CAPITAL CONCEPT TO REALIZE HOW A BUSINESS IS RUN

As part of her school project, Rhea decides to set-up a lemonade store in her residential society. What can such a school project teach her about how billion-dollar conglomerates run their businesses?

Understanding the Importance of Net Working Capital

While popular press cites sales and profits as the most important elements in a business, the real mettle of any good business is managing its net working capital. With poor net working capital management, companies can easily go bankrupt (e.g., Jet Airways, Kingfisher airlines). In addition, net working capital has a direct impact on the total return (or profit) a company makes. This is the main reason for automobile dealers being in the news for shutting down their operations due to unviable net working capital management.

Net Working Capital—The Concept

(As Figure 16.1 indicates, most complex businesses can be broken down into three to four broad boxes, that's it!)

Lemons supplier	Rhea's lemonade business	Consumers at her residential complex
• Local vendors that sell lemons to Rhea • Gives her a credit of 10 days—she can pay 10 days after buying it from the local vendor	• Rhea keeps an inventory of lemons and sugar for making lemonade • She makes the lemonade fresh on demand	• Rhea sells it to consumers in her residential complex • To keep up goodwill, she gives her end consumers a 15 day credit period—consumers can pay her 15 days after drinking lemonade

Figure 16.1: Value Chain Across Rhea's Lemonade Business. Maybe Rhea Should also Consider Changing the Name of Her Business. What Do You Think?

Net working capital, intuitively, implies the financial capital required to run her business. For instance, Rhea needs capital to keep an inventory of lemons and sugar. She also needs capital because she is giving her end consumers a line of credit. Her capital situation is assisted as she is getting a line of credit from her suppliers.

Her net working capital requirement in days = Credit she gives her end consumers + Inventory of lemons and sugar she has to keep – Credit she receives from her suppliers.

Inventory of lemons and sugar is expressed as days of sales of business. For instance, if her monthly business is ₹10,000 and she keeps an inventory of ₹1,000, then her inventory is 3 days (₹1,000 inventory/₹10,000 sales every month × 30 days in a month):

Net working capital for Rhea equals = 15 days (Credit she gives her end consumers) + 3 days (Her inventory in sales) – 10 days (Credit she receives from her suppliers) = 8 days of net working capital. This implies that she has to have a minimum capital ready of 8 days of business (8 days/30 days in a month × ₹10,000 monthly sales = ₹2,667).

In case she isn't able to provide this capital to run her business, her business will go bankrupt as end consumers will take their time to pay but input suppliers won't extend their credit line and she will have to shut her business down.

The more important implication of net working capital is the implication on profitability. Net working capital has a direct implication on return on investment (ROI) from a business:

Return on investment for Rhea = Profit/Sales × Sales/Investment.

As can be seen, sales/investment (net working capital is a proxy for investment in a simple business) has a direct implication for ROI. If she manages to reduce her investment (in Rupees or days), her ROI goes up. Intuitively, this translates to getting her to rotate her financial capital faster to earn a better return.

What Can Rhea Do to Improve Her Working Capital?

There are multiple levers Rhea can adopt to improve her working capital. For her purchases, she can look to enter long term contracts with her suppliers so that she gets a better line of credit from them. While negotiating, she can look to speak to multiple vendors so that she gets the most beneficial terms.

To manage her own inventory, she can look to forecast her demand correctly (e.g., do consumers come more often on a weekend morning rather than weekdays) to accurately forecast her inventory. She can look to see what inventory is easily available (e.g., salt) and stock less of it while keeping more amounts of the essential inventory (e.g., lemons).

For her end consumers, she can herself enter into long term contracts with key consumers to safeguard her business. She can also look to design her credit terms that is customized as per the profile of the end consumers, if the consumer buys more, they get a better price or a line of credit.

Where Can This Concept Be Applied?

This concept of net working capital to ascertain the capital required to stay in business or leveraging the concept to evaluate financial turns to determine ROI is used across all businesses. For example, it is the primary technique to evaluate the profitability of distributors across auto, FMCG and retail businesses. As the news of dealers in auto performing poorly emerges everywhere, leveraging net working capital is a concept that is extensively used to manage their profitability. This is also used in B2B businesses or service businesses.

In conclusion, while sales and profits are end metrics, the key metric to manage them is often net working capital and should be mastered accordingly to run a successful, sustainable business.

While we explored the concept of net working capital in this chapter to run a day-to-day business, the next chapter will explore the concept of net present value (NPV), should that business be run in the first place?

17

NPV: FOCUS ON THE NOW

Mia, a fresh MBA and a banker, is looking at three potential projects in front of her. The first project is an investment in an amusement park on the outskirts of the city, the second project is to invest in a coffee farm and the third project is to invest in a restaurant in Mumbai. She is confused as to which project she should look at. Her boss wants her to give him an answer by sunset.

Table 17.1 indicates the cash flows from each of the projects. A positive cash flow indicates an incoming cash flow to Mia's firm (which is good) while a negative cash flow indicates an outgoing cash flow out of Mia's firm (which is bad).

Project Name	At the Start	Year 1	Year 2	Year 3	Year 4
1. Amusement park	–25,000	0	2,000	1,200	33,000
2. Coffee farm	–400	100	125	150	200
3. Restaurant	–7,000	1,000	2,000	3,500	500

Table 17.1: For Each of the Projects, the Likely Cash Flows over the Next Few Years. Without Reading Any Further, What Does Your Gut Instinct Tell You? Which One Should You Put Your Money In?

50,000 Feet Definition

In one line, the NPV is the final monetary value of the project, as of today.

Key Concept

Discount Rate or Cost of Capital

Would you want to have ₹1,000 today or tomorrow? Would you have ₹1,000 today or after 10 years? You would want it today. Isn't it? Why?

The reason is simple. If you had the money today, you could invest it and get a return on that investment. This is known as the time value of money. The value of money reduces as you keep going into the future.

If you had to borrow money from a lender to invest in this project, you would have to pay the lender. This rate, indicated in %, is termed as the discount rate or the cost of capital. Any future cash flow is discounted (Divided by this percentage) to get the present value of this future cash flow.

Mathematically, present value of cash flow = Future value of cash flow/(1 + Cost of capital)$^{(No.\ of\ years)}$.

For instance, a cash flow of ₹1,000 after 3 years would be worth ₹751 (₹1000/(1 + 10%)^3) today.

Net Present Value

The NPV is the present value of all future cash flows. It is the monetary value of any project today. To calculate the NPV, all future cash flows are discounted by the appropriate cost of capital and the NPV is arrived at:

Mathematically, NPV = (Cash flow at the start) + (Incoming cash flow at year 1 – Outgoing cash flow at year 1)/(1 + Cost of capital) + (Incoming cash flow at year 2 – Outgoing cash flow at year 2)/(1 + Cost of capital)² + (Incoming cash flow at year 3 – Outgoing cash flow at year 3)/(1 + Cost of capital)³ and so on.

In the above example, the NPV for the three projects are:

For the amusement park, the NPV is:

NPV = –25,000 + 0 (No cash flow in year 1) + 2,000 (Incoming cash flow in year 2)/(1 + 10%)² + 1,200 (Incoming cash flow in year 3)/(1 + 10%)³ + 33,000 (Incoming cash flow in year 4)/(1 + 10%)⁴.

The NPV turns out to be 94. Similarly, the NPV for the Coffee Farm and the restaurant turn out to be 44 and –1,467, respectively. From a purely theoretical standpoint, any project with a positive NPV should be pursued. In this case, the amusement park and the coffee farm generate positive cash flows today and should be pursued. The project on the restaurant should be discontinued.

However, the interpretation isn't that simple. Between the amusement park and the coffee park, the amusement park is preferable as its NPV is higher. But in case of the amusement park, the major cash flow of 33,000 is happening in the fourth year. A significant cash flow in the period so far away can be a source of risk. In addition, it is extremely sensitive to the cost of capital assumed. If the cost of capital is assumed to be 12 per cent instead of 10 per cent, the NPV of the amusement park becomes –1,579, while the NPV of the coffee farm reduces marginally to 23.

In conclusion, the benefit of the NPV metric is that it is simple, easy to follow and can be computed easily in excel sheets. However, it is highly sensitive to the cost of capital rate assumed and doesn't give an indication of % profitability of the project.

In this case, Mia recommends both the positive NPV projects of the amusement park and the coffee farm. However, she prefers the lower NPV project, the coffee farm, because of its lower sensitively to the cost of capital assumptions and uniform incoming cash flow across years.

Once you have decided on which line of business to enter, you need to understand financial statements to assess if the business is running as per original plan. Enter the next set of chapters on financial statements.

Is That So?

1. Did you know that NPV is extensively used by Warren Buffett to evaluate new projects?
2. Did you know that NPV as a concept dates back to the 19th century?
3. Did you know that NPV started to become included in finance textbooks from the 1950s?

18

FINANCIAL STATEMENTS: THE KING AMONGST KINGS!

Sonia, an MBA graduate, after being inspired by the show Two Broke Girls *wants to open a bakery shop in Bandra West, Mumbai. Her brother tells her that understanding financial statements is critical. She is not sure why these stupid statements should come in the way of her realizing her dream and appearing in Bombay Times.*

Why Is This Chapter Important for You? Why Do Financial Statements Matter?

Why do businesses operate? Although they believe they are making the world a better place, unfortunately they operate to make money.

How do you measure if you are making money? By understanding and analysing financial statements.

Understanding and analysing financial statements is at the core of any management job. Irrespective of whether you want to open a bakery shop or manage a brand or become an Instagram sensation, a limited knowledge of financial statements is a massive handicap. To put this into perspective, even the drug lords of hit sitcoms like *Narcos* always have qualified professionals to interpret and analyse their financial statements.

So What Are Financial Statements?

Financial statements (refer to Table 18.1), or the ones that are most often used, come in three shapes and sizes—the profit and loss (P&L) statement, the balance sheet and the cash flow statement.

The P&L statement, the report mostly blurted out on news channels by excited journalists, is a statement on the revenue, costs and profit of the company over the previous quarter or the year.

The balance sheet is a statement on what the company owns (e.g., plants, cash, inventory) and what it needs to pay out (e.g., loans, equity of the owners).

The cash flow statement is a statement on the actual cash reserves of the company. If you don't have cash to run a business, your company goes bankrupt. Ask Lehman brothers.

Financial Statement	Description	Key Terms	Frequency
Profit and loss statement	Overview of revenue, cost and profit of the company	Revenue, Cost, Profit	Change over a time period, typically yearly or quarterly.
Balance sheet	Overview of all assets (e.g. plant, cash, inventory) and liabilities (e.g. debt to be paid) of the company	Assets, Liabilities, Equity	Report at a point in time
Cash flow statement	Report on actual cash the company has. Remember cash is king.	Cash flow from operating, financing and investing	Change over a time period, typically yearly or quarterly.

Table 18.1: Overview of the Three Financial Statements. Your Romantic Partner Is Unlikely to be Impressed If You Make a Mistake with These!

What Does a Bakery Shop Look Like?

Sonia, inspired by the hit TV series *Two Broke Girls*, wants to open a bakery shop in Bandra, Mumbai. Her bakery shop operations will resemble the chart shown in Figure 18.1.

| Market to buy raw material (e.g., sugar, wheat) | Employees working at the store | Customers at the store |

Figure 18.1: Typical Flow of Money across an Organization. Now You Know Where You Stand in the Corporate Chain

Sonia will buy her raw materials (e.g., sugar, wheat, milk) from the farmer's market. Some of these markets allow her to purchase on a credit period of 15 days. She will bring these to her kitchen at her store, which is rented, where her employees will bring these to life by converting them into mouth-watering pastries. Hopefully, word will spread far and wide, through some smart marketing, which will attract customers who will pay Sonia at the store. Let us look at how her financial statements stack up for her.

The profit and loss statement gives a view of her revenues, costs and profits at her bakery over a period of time.

Revenue = (No. of consumers × Bill size per consumer)

Revenue – Cost of goods sold (COGS) = Gross margin

Gross margin – Operating expenses including rent, employee cost and other administrative expenses = Operating Margin

Operating margin – Interest expenses and taxes = Net profit.

In Sonia's case, the revenue at her bakery shop is the actual sales that happens at her bakery shop, the consumers who come to buy at her shop and the price they pay for buying various cakes and pastries at her bakery. COGS refers to the cost of materials involved to make cakes and pastries, including dough, sugar and milk. Gross margin is arrived at once COGS is reduced from the revenue.

Operating expenses imply the expenses needed to operate the business including the rent she has to pay for the bakery, the salaries for the people she employs and cost of marketing about her new store. These expenses are often termed as selling, general and administrative costs (S, G and A). Also, don't forget the electricity and AC costs. Without these, all those pretty pastries will melt. Operating margin, also termed as EBITDA (Earnings before interest, tax, depreciation and amortization), is arrived at after reducing operating costs from gross margin. This is so bland, isn't it?

To arrive at final profit or the number that eventually matters, also termed as net profit, Sonia has to reduce the interests she has to pay on the loans she has taken to run her business and pay big brother, the government, taxes and arrive at net profit. In case Sonia doesn't have a rich daddy to keep funding her bakery shop, she has to carefully understand her net profit. To summarize, from the term EBITDA, Sonia has to remove 'ITDA' (Interest, tax, depreciation and amortization) to arrive at net profit.

Let us take an actual example to bring this mythical creature to life.

Key metrics to analyse a P&L statement include whether net margin is positive or not, obviously, and if it is growing from the previous quarter or year. In addition, three key profit measures are carefully looked at—gross margin, operating margin and net margin. All these terms are expressed as percentage of revenue and are compared to the previous quarter or year

Profit and Loss Statement Element	Value in ₹	Remarks
Revenue	10,000	If 100 consumers come to her bakery in the first year and each buys a pastry worth ₹100
Cost of goods sold	2,500	If it takes ₹25 as raw material cost (sugar, dough, milk) to make a ₹100 pasty. Multiply that by the number of consumers (100)
Gross margin	7,500 (75%)	Formulated as revenue—COGS. Also expressed as percentage of revenue
Rent	1,000	Rent Sonia has to pay to operate the bakery
Employee cost	2,000	Salary of the employees who work at her pastry store
Marketing cost	500	Cost of marketing material in her area
Operating margin	4,000 (40%)	Formulated as gross margin – rent – employee cost – marketing cost. Also expressed as percentage of revenue.
Interest cost	300	Interest cost Sonia has to pay for the loan she has taken

(continued)

(continued)

Profit and Loss Statement Element	Value in ₹	Remarks
Tax to the government	700	Tax Sonia has to pay to big brother
Depreciation	500	Depreciation implies machinery expense (2,500) is deducted over a 5 year period as it is assumed to be its life (Depreciation = 2,500/5)
Net margin	2,500 (25%)	Finally, what she earns! Will this feature her on *The Bombay Times*?

Table 18.2: The Profit and Loss Statement of Sonia's Bakery Store

or are compared to a nearby competitor. Sonia senses that her gross margin (75%), operating margin (40%) and net margin (25%) are better than her arch-rival from college, Neha, who is also running a bakery store. She decides to put up an appropriate message on Instagram to make Neha jealous.

The balance sheet provides Sonia with a view of what she owns and what she owes to others because of her bakery at a point in time.

An asset is something a company owns—a plant, equipment to run a plant, cash in hand, inventory of unsold goods and raw materials. A liability is something a company owes others—money payable to vendors, interest expenses on loans and so on.

The difference in what a company owns (assets) and what a company owes (liabilities) is termed as equity, translating to the net items that the owners of the bakery have for themselves after all dues have been paid out:

Assets (what a company owns) = Liabilities (what a company owes) + Equity (what is left for the owners).

In management circles, this equation is considered the holy grail of accounting. The universe can turn pink, but the above equation will be protected by an army of chartered accountants. There are a vicious number of business professionals and chartered accountants who will try to ensure that this equation holds good. To sound ubercool with the opposite gender, this equation is termed as the asset liability match.

In case of Sonia's business, this is how the balance sheet appears (refer to Tables 18.3 and 18.4).

The difference in Tables 18.3 and 18.4, assets and liabilities, is termed as equity, implying what is left for her (Table 18.5).

While there are many balance sheet ratios, the most important one is the debt to equity ratio. It is defined as the

Assets	Value	Remarks
Equipment at bakery store	2,500	Equipment to make the dough base and furniture to make the bakery look beautiful
Cash in hand	3,000	Cash to run daily operations
Inventory	2,000	Inventory at the bakery shop—raw materials and final pastries
Total	7,500	

Table 18.3: The Asset Component of the Balance Sheet of Sonia's Bakery Store

Liabilities	Value	Remarks
Amount payable to vendor	1,500	Sonia buys raw materials from the farmer's market on credit. This represents the amount that is payable to her raw material vendors.
Loans taken to fund business	3,000	Sonia has taken a loan to fund her bakery store.
Total	4,500	

Table 18.4: The Liabilities Component of the Balance Sheet of Sonia's Bakery Store

Equity	Value
Total assets	7,500
Total liabilities	4,500
Difference	3,000

Table 18.5: The Equity Component of the Balance Sheet of Sonia's Bakery Store

total liabilities to total equity. A number that is less than 1 is preferable. In case of Sonia's bakery:

Debt to equity ratio = Total liabilities (4500)/Total equity (3000) = 1.5.

The cash flow statement gives a view of where the company stands with respect to the ultimate king, which is cash.

The cash flow statement is one of the holy trinities in financial statements, after the profit loss and the balance sheet statements. In one line, it measures the actual cash a company has at the end of a financial period.

Cash is always the king in running a business as it is a measure of a firm's ability to run its immediate day-to-day operations and not go bankrupt. It is different from the P&L statement as a P&L uses accrual accounting while the cash flow statement is a measure of actual cash. Please do not worry if the above statement sounds like your boss praising you.

For instance, if a service is delivered to a customer with a credit period of five months, the revenue will be recognized when the service is delivered but the cash will be recognized in the cash flow statement only when the cash from the customer comes in. Similarly, if a firm has to pay its vendors and has a credit period of three months from the vendors, it is recognized as an expense in the P&L statement when it buys, but it reflects in the cash flow statement only when the cash is paid out.

Needless to say, a positive cash flow is generally seen as a good thing while a negative cash flow is seen as a source of concern. If a firm's cash flow is negative because it is actively investing, it may be considered alright but if it is negative without aggressive investment but poor operations, it is a huge source of concern.

There are three types of cash flows—cash flow from operations, cash flow from investments and cash flow from financing activities (refer to Figure 18.2). The addition of all these three cash flows is the total cash a company holds at a period in time.

Cash flow from operations is an indication of the actual cash the core business is making and is the most important metric in financial statements.

Cash flow from operations indicates the core cash a business generates. This metric is critical as cash is necessary to run any business. A company can easily go bankrupt if it doesn't have cash to run a business to pay for items like salaries, interest cost, amount owed to vendors and so on.

Cash flow from operations	Cash flow from investment	Cash flow from financing
- Cash flows from routine business activities - Different from net profit as it reconciles non-cash transactions (blah!)	- Cash flows to growth future business by increasing assets - Cash flows from capital expenditure like buying plant, property and equipment	- Cash flow from financing activities to grow alternate businesses or generate capital to grow existing business - Cash flows from raising debt, paying out dividends or investment equity

Figure 18.2: An Overview of the Various Forms of Cash Flow. Always Remember, Cash Is King. In Case You Don't Believe It, Try Not Paying Your Monthly EMI for a Month

Mathematically, cash from operations is defined as:

Cash flow from operations = Net income + Change from the previous year of non-cash items (Depreciation + Accounts payable – Accounts receivable).

Cash flow from operations (refer to Table 18.6) starts with the net income. This is the final number in the P&L statement. It adds on elements that are non-cash related but have been used to arrive at the net income in the P&L statement.

Depreciation is an accounting deduction in the P&L and not an actual cash expense, hence it is added back. Similarly, accounts payable, due to a credit period given, has been factored in earlier in the balance sheet but the company hasn't paid money to the vendors yet, so it is sitting on incremental cash. Accounts receivable from consumers is deducted as this is accounted for in the financial statements but the cash hasn't been received from the consumers, due to the credit period offered to consumers.

Cash from operations at the beginning of the previous year	0	She started her business this year and hence her cash flow from operations balance last year was nil
Net income	2,500	This is the last item in Sonia's profit and loss statement
Depreciation	500	Depreciation implies machinery expense (2,500) is deducted over a 5 year period as it is assumed to be its life. This element is

(continued)

THE PRACTICAL MBA

		reported in the profit and loss statement. It is being added back as it is a non-cash accounting transaction deducted in the profit and loss statement and hence it is added back to the cash flow statement.
Accounts payable	1,500	Amount payable to vendors but hasn't been paid yet as Sonia receives a credit line. This item is reported in the balance sheet.
Accounts receivable	0	Amount to be received from consumers, if any
Inventory	–2,000	It is negative as cash has been spent to increase inventory of materials and pastries. This item is reported in the balance sheet.
Cash flow from operations at the end of this year	2,500	

Table 18.6: The Cash Flow from Operations for Sonia's Bakery

Cash flow from investing primarily indicates building capital expenditure—plant, property and equipment.

Cash flow from investing implies investing capital to grow an existing business. It is primarily seen as investing in capital expenditure—plant, property and equipment. The money that is generated from cash flow from operations is generally used for investing in future growth of the same business.

In case of Sonia's business, if she decides to buy machinery worth 500 to grow her existing business, her cash flow from investing will be –500 for the year. It is negative as it is a cash outflow.

Cash flow from financing indicates debt taken to fund growth or new equity issued by a company to increase capital inflows.

Financing activities indicates raising money from capital markets to fund growth in existing business or setting up a new business. In case a company takes on debt, the cash flow from financing increases as debt implies a cash inflow. In case a company issues more equity, it implies a cash inflow as more capital is coming in. In case a firm pays out dividends to its owners, it implies a cash flow expense:

Cash flow from financing = Debt taken during the year + Equity issued during the year – Dividends paid out to shareholders.

In case of Sonia's business, she has taken 3,000 as debt during the year to fund her bakery business. Her cash flow from financing stands at 3,000 for the year. It is positive as it is a cash inflow.

The total cash flow balance at the end of a period is the sum of the three cash flows—cash flow from operations, investing and financing and the cash flow balance at the beginning of the previous year:

Total cash flow balance at the end of this year = Total cash flow balance at the end of the previous year + Cash flow from operations during this year + Cash flow from investing during this year + Cash flow from investing during this year.

In summary, cash is the king and rightfully so. The smart analyst always studies the cash flow statement first to see if

Cash flow balance at the end of the previous year	0	She started her business this year and hence her cash flow balance last year was nil
Cash flow from operations	2,500	
Cash flow from investing	–500	It is negative as it is a cash outflow
Cash flow from financing	3,000	It is positive as it is a cash inflow
Total cash flow balance at the end of this year	5,000	Total cash in hand for Sonia. Yay!

Table 18.7: The Total Cash Flow Balance at the End of the Year for Sonia. Pretty Neat, Isn't It?

the total cash a company has is increasing or not. In case it isn't, it should send off warning signals straightaway.

In conclusion, understanding the financial statements of a company are absolutely critical to assess where a company stands and evaluate the health of your company. Without being comfortable with these is equivalent to a cricketing batsman not knowing how to play the short-pitched ball.

Is That So?

1. Did you know that Satyam, Enron and WorldCom have found themselves in the midst of accounting fraud leading to high-profile arrests?
2. Did you know that a company's board of directors are expected to sign off on a company's annual reports when they are released?

3. Did you know that if you buy one single share of a company, you will be entitled to receive a 300-page colour print out of a company's annual report? In all likelihood, the printout and the courier cost of that document will be two to three times the share price of that company.

(As a younger version of myself, I would often buy one share of the many blue chip companies so as to get invited to their annual general meet. My interest in attending the annual general meeting would not be to learn about the company but to devour the fantastic multi-course meal that was on offer. In my opinion, the multi-course meal at Infosys' annual general meeting is probably the best.)

19

ENTERPRISE VALUE: HOW MUCH DO I NEED TO PAY TO TAKEOVER APPLE?

Ishant, an investment banker, has been asked the unthinkable. In case his investment bank wants to finance the hostile takeover of Apple, how much would they need to finance this takeover of the century?

In simple English, he has to calculate a mystical term called enterprise value.

Enterprise value, as the name suggests, is an indication of how much a company is worth or how much you should pay if you were to buy the company today.

It is calculated as:

Enterprise value = Market capitalization + Debt (Short term + Long term) – Cash.

Enterprise value is seen as an alternative to market capitalization (no. of shares outstanding × price per share) as it is provides a complete picture of the company you want to buy. It is complete as it captures the debt a company has and the cash it has in hand. Debt, both short and long term, is added to market capitalization in this calculation as you automatically have to pay that debt back if you were to buy this company. Cash is deducted in the enterprise value calculation as when you buy that company, you can use the cash to pay off the debt.

How Is Enterprise Value Used?

Enterprise value is often used by financial investors when they are looking to evaluate the value of a company in case they want to purchase it. In a lot of hostile corporate takeovers, enterprise value is often seen as one of the main metrics to evaluate.

In addition, it is also used by financial analysts to evaluate the company health. The specific ratios that are used include:

Enterprise value/Sales
Enterprise value/EBITDA

Enterprise value/Sales gives an indication of how the company is valued with respect to day-to-day sales while Enterprise value/EBITDA indicates how the company is valued with respect to its day-to-day profit. These ratios are used as benchmarks across companies to compare operations. For instance, in FMCG, it is considered that if Enterprise Value/Sales is 3, it is a healthy valuation while if the Enterprise Value/EBITDA is 15, it is a healthy valuation.

So How Much Does Ishant Need to Pay for Apple?

Apple's enterprise value has been hovering around $1.4 trillion. That is how much you need to pay to become the complete owner of Apple. So start saving up from your monthly salary to get there.

In conclusion, understanding enterprise value is critical to decipher net worth of companies to make investment choices.

ENTREPRENEURSHIP

BUILDING THE NEXT BIG THING

It is the ultimate statement of success and self-realization to build your own firm and see it succeed. The joy, thrill, glamour and money that result from a successful journey are unmatchable. However, it should be known that majority of entrepreneurs fail and the journey towards a successful start-up is miserable from a lifestyle perspective. In addition, it is the wrong motive to pursue your own journey in case you don't like your boss or have been laid off. Unless of course you have a great idea and the ability to see it go live. This section gives you a hands-on view on what to expect in your journey as an entrepreneur.

66

*A fool and his money are lucky enough
to get together in the first place.*
Michael Douglas
as Gordon Gekko in the movie
Wall Street

*My son is now an 'entrepreneur'. That's what
you're called when you don't have a job.*
Ted Turner
founder of Donald Trump's
favourite news network *CNN*

99

20

BUILDING YOUR OWN UNICORN

The decision to take the ultimate plunge to build your own firm is never an easy one.[16] The decision can be spurred in a moment of realizing a path-breaking idea or an intense desire for individual freedom driven by a stifling corporate culture. Whatever the reason, the path is akin to a game of thorns where the entire world seems to queue up against you. This chapter intends to serve as a primer for aspiring entrepreneurs to help them navigate through the initial days before the real battle begins!

Build a Great Product at the Right Place, Time and Cost

It is a no-brainer that you need to have a potential idea that solves a genuine pain point for end consumers. The pain point is termed as genuine if at least a million consumers feel it (not just a few consumers on 80 feet road, Koramangala, Bangalore) and are ready to pay for it. By paying, it implies an amount that makes unit economics positive. While this idea of yours is getting prototyped, it is advisable to not rock your existing job or source of stable cash flow. The disruption to your steady cash flow is advisable only when your great idea has successfully been piloted.

Nothing Makes the World Go Around Like Money

The initial capital to start your venture, termed as seed capital, is often generated from your own pocket or from well-wishers. Once you are able to show a certain traction in consumer usage scale, aspiring entrepreneurs typically approach venture capitals for further funding or additional funding. Each subsequent round of funding is designated by a letter in the alphabet series (Series A, B, C, D, etc). For instance, Flipkart has had over 15 rounds of financing having raised in excess of $7 bn.[17] During each of these stages in funding, venture capital investors assess the potential valuation of the company through a due-diligence process. To witness a dramatic version of this process, you might want to watch a few episodes of the hit sitcom *Shark Tank*. Although securing a funding is considered the gold standard for an aspiring entrepreneur, as your grandparents would advise, it is best advisable to attempting to scale up with your own limited capital without relinquishing control.

It Is All in the Name

The importance of this step can never be adequately emphasized. A good catchy name for your start-up is necessary to resonate with end consumers and investors. The general guideline for having an attractive name includes having around two to three syllables (e.g., Google, Amazon, Flipkart) and not more than that (avoid Dhronacharya Pratap Singh Associates & Company). Needless to say, any name that sounds young (e.g., Apple) is better than an older sounding name. The critical step is to check if someone else is using the desired name and blocking it if it is available. This step can be accomplished on the MCA 21 (Ministry of Company Affairs) website.

Stay Fully Involved, Stay Foolish

Although it is important to stay fully committed and passionate to your start-up, it is sensible to be legally sound and protected. The business structure of your start-up needs to be agreed upon at the very start to avoid unforeseen future debacles. The most primitive version is the sole proprietorship model where you are the eventual owner with every revenue and cost item hitting your personal wealth. As a consequence, you are individually liable for all losses to your firm. This structure is advisable for freelancers who do not have significant cost liabilities while operating your businesses. A safer version of a business structure, termed by some as the greatest invention of the previous century, is the limited liability partnership model. As the name suggests, the model guarantees you access to the entire revenue and profits while limiting your losses to the invested capital. As a result, your personal wealth that is not invested in your company is deemed safe.

Get a 21st Century Garage Space to Start Work

While entrepreneurs in the previous century were famous for working in their garages before making it big, the 21st century has made it easier for aspiring entrepreneurs to get a physical space. The ever-mushrooming co-working spaces (e.g., WeWork, Innov8), with desks and rooms for rent with all other services taken care of (e.g., internet, cleaning, security, cafeteria, parking), are an extremely attractive proposition for aspiring entrepreneurs. The cost of such services is fairly reasonable with an individual desk costing between 8,000 and 12,000 a month while a dedicated meeting room costing between 15,000 and 20,000 a month.

The Paperwork Is Not as Messy but Necessary

Registering your company is a necessary evil. It involves obtaining a DIN (director identification number), filing the certificate of incorporation at the MCA website, obtaining a permanent account number, tax account number, registering for Goods and Services Tax (GST), blocking the company name among other steps. In case a patent is involved for your product, it involves a few more days. To be reasonably practical, the entire process of registering your start-up can take around three weeks including the time you require to get the documents ready.

Make Your Friends on Social Media Jealous

Even before you have decided to take the plunge and register your firm, a social media presence to test the concept and user interest can be of great help. In terms of effectiveness of media, Facebook is passé while Instagram is the new king of commerce. Not to forget, leveraging LinkedIn for understanding end user traction is picking up. More than product testing, a following of at least 10,000 people on your product pages is a handy start. To pay for followers or likes is not advisable, they rarely end up subscribing to your product. An organic following is always advisable in the beginning before driving up an audience by paying for them.

Choose the Right Backbone in Form of the Technical Infrastructure

Given most contemporary start-ups are technology-enabled platforms, employing the right technical infrastructure can be critical in the beginning. Technical infrastructure is required to store critical user data on cloud servers, generating user behaviour insights through an analytical engine, sending promotional e-mails to end users or employing the latest security firewalls to avoid breach of data (remember

Facebook?). While software as a service (SaaS) based on a pay per use model is provided by many vendors, Amazon Web Services (AWS) is a great starting point for start-ups of any size.

Soft Infrastructure, in Terms of People, Is Equally Important

Working at a start-up can be very unglamorous in the beginning as you are everything from the CEO to the chaprasi. However, it is important to think of your core team as you plan to start your company. Key considerations for getting members to join your core team are based on personal chemistry and only then complementarity of skill sets. In case you are not sure of the importance of this step, I would request you to watch the movie *The Social Network* based on the initial days of Facebook.

Professional and Social Support Is the Most Important Step in the Process

Given starting your own venture is a once in a lifetime and a very demanding process, reaching out to professionals who have done it before might be of great help. There are numerous resources available online to assist aspiring entrepreneurs in their day-to-day transactions. Biographies of leading entrepreneurs (e.g., *The Everything Store* [Amazon], *Steve Jobs* [Apple]) is a great account of the emotional and mental struggles an entrepreneur goes through. In addition, there are incubators with experts that provide live assistance (e.g., NSRCEL in IIM Bangalore). Assistance provided from incubators can range from professional coaching, providing physical space to contacts of key customers or financiers. What is equally important is a strong social support for an aspiring entrepreneur. The journey of starting your own company is gruelling and lonely, and support from family and friends is absolutely necessary.

In conclusion, as exhilarating as it may sound, starting your own firm is a very difficult job, both emotionally and physically. The above list is a very good starting point to build the Silicon Valley of your dreams. In the next chapter, we explore a corollary to this chapter on why entrepreneurs fail.

21 | WHY ENTREPRENEURS FAIL

These days, it is becoming a norm to start you own firm.[18] From four start-ups a day in India, the day is not far when we will move to one start-up an hour. However, as is well known, more than 90 per cent of start-ups fail to make an impact.[19]

Here is a checklist for every aspiring entrepreneur on the pitfalls to avoid while creating his/her own dream business empire.

It Was a Bad Idea. Duh!

It is a very bad idea when a product that worked in China or the United States is blindly emulated for India. Unless of course, it is solving a genuine pain point. Over the last decade, ideas which have seen traction include organizing unorganized daily services, namely, commute, grocery shopping, domestic help, shoe cleaning, cable TV and home broadband going forward. The moot point is that cute products that don't address a genuine pain point won't work. For instance, will you pay even a rupee for an app that enables you to add cute emoticons on an existing image?

Scale or Rather Lack of It

The single biggest design flaw is to make a product that is relevant only for people staying in 100 feet road in Indiranagar. If a product cannot be consumed by 10 million users (Yes, 10 million), then it is likely to be unprofitable and incapable of making large-scale impact. Scale is necessary as business profits tend to rise disproportionately with rising efficiencies of consumer scale. In case you are not comfortable with scale, a personality-oriented start-up might work for you (e.g., a tuition centre) but it isn't sustainable beyond a few years.

Negative Unit Economics

This should ideally be the first and not the third tenet. Unit economics or profit per consumer should be the principal metric when evaluating a business idea. In case it is negative, a business should not be initiated. Irrespective of how lofty valuations of Uber and Lyft might seem on the stock exchanges, an idea with negative unit economics is bound to fail. Either the financial investor will drive out the owner or the cash guzzling start-up of yours will meet its organic end. Numerically, any start-up that cannot generate a return on capital employed of at least 10–12 per cent in the first three to five years should be carefully avoided. Instead, the money should be invested in capital markets to generate a relatively assured return without the emotional vagaries of running your own start-up.

Treat Consumers as an Afterthought

While I can give you a theoretical discourse on consumer experience, let me give you a live example to make my point. A leading food technology company recently changed its food delivery policy. If the delivery boy calls you while delivering food and you happen to miss the call for a reason, they will take the food back, charge the entire 100 per cent of the amount you have paid as cancellation fee and send you a reprimanding message that you should be more responsible with food as a consumer. This policy is wrong at so many levels, a 100 per cent cancellation fee for missing a phone call is outright unfair to a consumer, the model assumes every delivery boy is operating with the heart of an angel and that you as a consumer will do nothing else in life but wait for their call. It is not surprising that this policy has led to massive angst online and it is only a matter of time before the food technology company has to answer some very tough questions on consumer attrition to their financial investors.

Societal Pressures—The *Log Kya Kahenge* Syndrome

Urban India has liberalized a lot towards its attitudes on pursuing your own start-up but we still have a long way to go. A plush cushy job with an MNC (multinational corporation) is still seen as the most desirable option with appropriate societal cushion. In case you don't agree, try telling the grumpy father of the beautiful lady you are wooing, '*I am an entrepreneur. I create jobs and wealth. I am the founder of Toshniwal and Zaveriwala enterprises*'. Imagine what the aunty in your neighbourhood will do to you at every kitty party in your house!

On a more serious note, being an entrepreneur is a very difficult job. You will have more bad days than good ones. It is a very lonely and depressing journey. The brutal work hours that accompany the profession inevitably take a toll on your health and personal life. The best way to avoid energy sapping characters is to choose your social circles appropriately.

Poor Choice of Initial Team

The first 5 to 10 members will go a long way in determining the probability of success of your start-up. If you get a bunch of micromanaging, artificial pressure creating maniacs, you are better served trying to request your old boss to give you your old cushy job back.

The initial team will need to have trust and respect amongst each other for smooth functioning. A leading online housing portal had their founder arguing with their investors like petty teenage girls on an everyday basis giving stiff competition to Ekta Kapoor's serials. We all know how that saga ended. To avoid egos flaring up unnecessarily, it is best advisable that every member in the founding team brings a different functional skill set. Too many people doing the same job is bound to create friction and unnecessary stress.

Luck

It is an age-old adage that you make your own luck; the harder you work, the luckier you get. But despite all the good intentions, there is an element of karmic destiny that takes over. You have to be at the right place at the right time like billionaire entrepreneurs Bill Gates and Jeff Bezos have both mentioned over the years. In case of Amazon, Jeff Bezos has been quoted as saying that it was an incredible combination of starship, a once in a lifetime alignment. Not everyone is destined to be a magazine cover hopping, jet setting, president fighting, billionaire entrepreneur. Sometimes you should just live with that.

In conclusion, your start-up may or may not succeed. However, if the aforementioned tenets are ignored, it is bound to fail.

In the real world, a good entrepreneur is an excellent storyteller. In the next chapter, we look at how the best in the business, read movie scriptwriters, actually construct plots.

22

WRITING A BUSINESS MOVIE SCRIPT

Storytelling is an extremely important skill for our species. As numerous studies and books (e.g., *Sapiens*) have written about, stories have the power to capture the human imagination and can be attributed as one of the main reasons of domination of the human species.[20]

From the perspective of a corporate career, storytelling has far reaching consequences in bringing a workforce together through a common organizational vision or in developing impactful material to communicate to your consumers via mass media or in person. This chapter elaborates the techniques used by real storytellers, creative writers of movies and business sitcoms. As the next few paragraphs elaborate, the tools developed by cinematic scriptwriters can be heavily leveraged upon by corporate professionals.

Understand Your End Reader

Modern-day scriptwriting pivots around understanding the end reader. As part of this process, the end reader is carefully defined demographically in terms of age, gender, type of residence, economic affluence and proficiency in English. In addition, behavioural patterns are carefully defined like place of reading or watching the movie or sitcom (a flight or a weekend or in the morning on way to office), time taken to read or watch (at one go, in breaks, in groups or alone), preferred length of the book (less than 300 pages, 500 plus pages), purchase of buying the book (online, book store, borrow from a library). While it is difficult to accurately develop all of the above, a good visual thought of the end

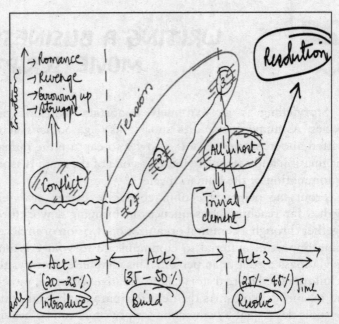

Figure 22.1: A Visual Depiction of How Movie Scripts Are Written. Pardon My Handwriting but I Hope You Get the Larger Message.

PS: A Lot of People Still Think My Handwriting Is Pretty Darn Good!

reader often results in a script that is powerfully aligned to the end reader's lifestyle.

In business parlance, the above exercise is called consumer segmentation and it is the cornerstone of any marketing team worth its salt.

Construct Kingly Content

Contrary to common perception, writing an actual business drama is more an analytical process rather than a creative one. The principal element of any story is the conflict, for romantic stories it resolves around boy meeting girl, boy liking girl, boy losing girl while for dramas it revolves around an ageing business legend losing his wealth and looking to make a comeback (*The Dark Knight Rises*) or a charismatic lawyer trying to precede over innumerable odds to win a case for his client (Harvey Spectre in *Suits*).

Any manuscript is divided into three acts (refer to Figure 22.1), Act 1 constitutes about 20–25 per cent of the manuscript focusing on introducing the key conflict, Act 2 constitutes about 45–50 per cent of the manuscript focusing on building the conflict while Act 3 focuses on resolving the conflict. A key element in any business drama revolves around developing the protagonist. A quick study of successful protagonists of hit drama sitcoms (*Suits*, *House*, *Mentalist*, *House of Cards*, *House of Lies*) enlists some common character traits—male, brilliant, charismatic, powerful orator, anti-establishment, emotionally challenged, romantically unsuccessful, unresolved issues from childhood. Most successful leads are constructed in the above way to build an adequate story around resolution of hidden inner conflict (Gregory House saving every patient, Harvey Spectre winning every legal case, Patrick Jane finding every murderer, Walter White often taking the morally correct route despite being a drug dealer).

There are certain tricks that are employed to make a story gripping. As part of building the conflict in Act 2, there are often three incidents of failures of the lead protagonist extensively referred to. At each of the three incidents of failures, it seems that progress is being made but the lead protagonist fails miserably and at the end of the third failure, it seems all is lost (In change management parlance, this phase is also called 'depths of despair'). In case of *The Dark Knight Rises*, Christian Bale loses to his adversary a couple of times despite gaining his physical strength and all seems lost at the third contact when he is pushed down a deep well. In case of *House*, there are three sets of treatments which he prescribes but they all fail after showing initial improvements and the patient is on the verge of complete collapse at the end of the third failure. In such a scenario, the writer often resorts to a 'trivial element' to leapfrog the protagonist back into the race. *House* often saves his patients by remembering a water cooler conversation with his best friend while Christian Bale is told of an anecdote of a young boy who climbed out a deep well. In our very own *3 Idiots*, it was a spare generator which Aamir Khan had created during one of his classes that is used to help Kareena Kapoor's sister see through her pregnancy.

The oft repeated trick in a drama story is to introduce a few twists at the end. In *Sixth Sense*, Bruce Willis realizes he is not alive through the whole sequence while most of Leonardo De Caprio's movies over the last few years revolve around his mental health and associated twists with it.

Tighten It and Pack a Punch!

Once the draft manuscript of a business drama is ready, it becomes necessary to pack a punch and make the script as fast paced as possible. To achieve this objective, the principle of minimalism is heavily leveraged. As part of this principle, each line of the manuscript is deleted, and an evaluation is made on whether the resulting script stands on its own or falls flat. In case the script stands, the line is deleted as it seems redundant and in case the script falls, the line is retained as it is absolutely necessary. Such a rigorous exercise conducted on every line of the manuscript results in a fast-paced, water-tight script.

In a business environment, a similar exercise can be employed to tighten and pack a punch in communication with customers.

In conclusion, the power of effective storytelling can never be adequately emphasized. Given our species has outmanoeuvred all other species on the basis of this powerful paradigm, it is only imperative that this philosophy is consciously ingrained in a corporate professional. So the next time you watch an episode of *Suits* or *Billions* or a business movie, do watch it proudly rather than with an inherent sense of guilt.

In the following addendum, we explore how the principles of movie scriptwriting can be adapted to storytelling in day-to-day business.

Storytelling in Day-to-Day Business

According to the book *Sapiens*, one of the major reasons why our species has outmanoeuvred other species is its ability to narrate powerful stories and create a shared vision. Even today, in corporate careers, storytelling is a powerful tool in presenting your content in an engaging style in a large discussion, narrating an interesting business case, having superior appraisal discussions or generating a buy-in from your associated shareholders. In fact, there is so much noise in office, that storytelling is the only avenue left to separate someone from the crowd. Unfortunately, we are all taught to be numerically precise by parroting like zombies with a number punctuating every second word in our communication.

This primer looks at some of the leading principles deployed by movies and ad films that can be leveraged upon in day-to-day complicated communication.

Narrate the pain point clearly—the clearer it is, the more powerful the communication will be.

In the romantic world of movies and ad films, conflict identification is of paramount importance. Typical conflicts are along lines of boy meets girl, boy loses girl or a revenge family drama or a story of growing up for the lead protagonist. In business, a powerful story involves a clear identification of conflict or struggle. In contemporary times, usual conflicts include the need to transform or be wiped out, the incumbent losing market share or the incumbent being the #2 or the #3 player in a 'winner takes all' industry. In sophisticated business enclaves, this pain point is also termed as the burning platform.

Anecdotal communication is more powerful than robotic delivery of numbers.

Short snippets of information narrated as anecdotes or incidents are way more powerful than delivering an equivalent insight with seven numbers in every sentence. For instance, an anecdotal representation along lines of, '*I met Lakshmi enterprises, our largest distributor. The owner mentioned that we are not engaging with them in non-monetary ways which is fairly important to them and hence they were feeling a disconnect*' is more powerful than, '*Our primary research with 75 distributors and secondary research of 5 industry leading reports indicates that engagement is the #3 most important buyer value for our distributors with a top of mind recall of 63 per cent. Benchmarking on this third most important buyer value indicates we are in the 70th–80th percentile of our competitors*'.

The impact of such powerful snippets lies in its ability to get narrated and re-quoted in other forums and hence building a powerful organization level communication. In addition, leveraging anecdotes don't imply compromising on numerical rigour as the anecdote brings the numerical trend to life. In fact, no form of communication should leave an audience with more than five to seven numbers. The human brain will struggle to process more than that and will end up treating numerical rigour as an academic exercise after that.

Ironically, minimalism has exaggerated benefits.

The best of drama-cantered movies leverage the principle of minimalism during narration. Every second in a movie is deleted and then carefully evaluated if the rest of the movie still stands. If the movie still stands, the second is considered unnecessary and deleted. This results in a narration that is superfast-paced and highly engaging. No one appreciates movies that are garrulous like your boss.

Every spoken or written communication should engage this principle of minimalism. If a sentence or slide is unnecessary, it should be ruthlessly eliminated. The resulting communication will result in a narration that an audience will never lose interest in.

Highlight the resolution with an equal dosage of functional and emotional benefits.

In any movie or an ad film, a resolution to the identified conflict is of paramount importance. A resolution need not always be good (e.g., the Oscar winning movie *Parasite*). Like in ad films, a robust resolution in business involves a healthy mix of functional and emotional benefits. For instance, *an iPhone promises an emotional benefit of status and youth while it provides for a functional benefit of a superior camera, a superfast processor and a safe ecosystem.* In corporate careers, functional benefits revolve around resurgence in sales and costs while emotional benefits revolve around culture transformation and long-term sustainability benefits.

Leverage Calvin and Hobbes to come to the rescue.

Written communication is also important in powerful storytelling. Powerful tools involve using cartoon sketches, typically Calvin and Hobbes, to illustrate a pain point. *(Well, I could have provided a link for this, but I think you can google this for yourself.)*

This is useful as it deploys dry humour in conveying a controversial message. Also, powerful written communication involves painting the 'before' and 'after' images clearly. The most important tool I have often seen being deployed to convey powerful stories is to leave an audience with five sentences you want them to go back with.

Watch a lot of YouTube junk and sports entertainment to learn from the best.

The key question is, how do you get better at storytelling? The answer is very simple, learn from the best. Politicians with mass following are incredibly talented at storytelling. In addition, product launches of consumer electronics companies (think Apple) consciously narrate incredible stories. Finally, if you are in the mood, you should follow how stories are built in sports entertainment (e.g., wrestling). Watching their videos is a great way to having a free master class in storytelling.

In conclusion, leadership is about storytelling. While it is a lot of art, consciously practising along the lines mentioned above is highly instrumental in making someone successful and building image capital in the form of charisma.

As we talk extensively about storytelling, a discussion on storytellers and alternate careers cannot be far behind. Read on.

23

NEW-AGE SLASH CAREERS

It can be surprising to see hard-nosed, money-obsessed, promotion-focused IIM graduates trying to delve in the innovative world of creative arts.[21] The charm of writing, dancing, television commentary, photography, travel jockeying and other niche careers are catching up really fast. Given the opportunity cost of time and capital, these professions are extremely risky with a ridiculously high degree of failure. Yet, the thrill of doing something close to your heart is driving many in this direction. To manage this risk, many IIM graduates are tapping their network, building a critical mass and discovering newer channels as part of their own business model to crack this innovative genre.

Numerous IIM graduates have begun to dive in the field of creative arts.

Many outgoing IIM batches have at least one published author. Multiply that with the number of IIMs and you can guess the number of potential authors in the system ready to dive into the world of writing. If you look at the Indian fiction section in any modern bookstore, it is dominated with books by fresh IIM graduates. Over the last few years, a small but steadily increasing set of people are entering fields like photography, radio and travel jockeying, television commentary, movie direction and so on. In fact, there are many who have given up their steady careers to build a training school for these creative talents. However, for one Harsha Bhogle, there are thousands that fail to even make a mark.

The monetary payout in these professions is paltry, to be polite.

Newspapers are ripe with stories of Amish Tripathi's USD 1 million advance or Chetan Bhagat's royalty from movies that are adapted from his books. Especially in the case of the publishing industry, royalties and margins for young authors are paltry, if not embarrassing. Royalty from sold books are in the range of 7–10 per cent of MRP. A book selling 5,000 copies, termed as a domestic bestseller, priced at ₹299 will earn the author a royalty of ₹150,000 only. In all likelihood, it will be lesser than the monthly pay cheque of most fresh IIM graduates. Payouts in other associated professions are marginally better. An entry level Radio Jockey makes around ₹25,000–40,000 per month while a wildlife photographer makes an amount not very different. In summary, relying solely on a career in creative arts is monetarily unrewarding in the first few years. It is always advisable to run both careers in parallel before diving in full time. In Ravi Subramanian's own words, '*Writing is my hobby. If I give up my job to become a writer I will write because I have to write and not because I want to create. One is my bread but the other is my butter.*'

As expected, many IIM graduates are developing their own business model to monetize their ability.

Although monetarily unrewarding in the first few years, most graduates enter into the world of creative arts as it proves to be more satisfying rather than adding millions to a billion-dollar income statement. Many aspiring creatively oriented graduates are finding out innovative ways to rake in the moolah. The trend of self-publishing or publishing via Amazon Kindle is on the rise as royalties are significantly higher in these channels (over 70% of MRP). Wedding photographers and travel jockeys actively tap their alumni network to get a foothold into these alien industries. In addition, an active usage of the digital medium is seeing many trying to generate substantial impressions. Getting 10,000 likes on Facebook and numerous retweets on Twitter are passé. Creatively oriented graduates are pitching live to millions on channels like YouTube and Instagram. Some are even taking up part-time careers at coaching institutes to sustain themselves in the first few years of their struggle.

Over the last two years, there are other new age slash careers that have been making the news. Digital influencers are coming to the forefront, either by turning into motivational speakers on YouTube, teaching on their own audio podcast channel or increasingly delving into the world of beautifully cooked dishes and running an ecosystem around that on Instagram.

In conclusion, making a full-fledged career in creative arts is risky at best. Reaching the levels of success which Harsha Bhogle, Mallika Sarabhai or Rashmi Bansal have attained can be extremely rewarding. Similar to the movies, for every superstar, there are thousands who haven't made it. Giving up a full time monetarily rewarding career for an aspirational career in the creative arts is fraught with risk. A balancing act in the initial years is highly recommended before the career in the creative arts takes off at escape velocity.

24

FORECASTING THE NEXT DECADE

As we enter the new decade, it is interesting to reflect on the decade gone by.[22] The biggest facet of the previous decade has been the rise of entrepreneurship in driving career options and changing the lives of consumers like you and I. The previous decade has been characterized by the birth of nearly 20 unicorns, cash guzzling and struggling for profitability due to mind-boggling consumer discounts, employing millions as part of the gig economy and in some cases, ugly battles and lucrative exits for the founders. This chapter looks at how our lives as consumers changed over the decade gone by and the likely changes in the upcoming decade.

The biggest theme that emerged in the previous decade was the attempt made by entrepreneurs to organize day-to-day unorganized services based on rising internet penetration and providing assets as a service.

As a household, we organized all our unorganized services and shifted them online. It started with buying books online as books were standardized products with limited prices preventing any undue surprises. Then came the miraculous rise of apparel in e-commerce. Apparel was considered to be a difficult category because of intrinsic consumer needs of fit, texture and the desire to touch and feel from the end consumer. However, due to a great shopping experience, exclusive online deals and ridiculous consumer discounts, we shopped at Myntra, Jabong and Amazon.

With most household spends going online, it was a matter of time before groceries went online too. Bigbasket innovated in this category by offering specific delivery slots and offering a wide portfolio. Groceries, however, is a complex animal.

Despite the incredible rise of e-commerce, it constitutes at best 2–3 per cent of the entire category with local *kirana* (grocery) stores constituting 85–87 per cent of the total category with Modern Trade accounting for the rest.[23] One of the reasons for this is consumers still buy fresh vegetables from the local *kirana* store while banking on e-commerce for branded goods. In addition, we ate online with Swiggy, driven by the experience and the discounts. Although there were trade protests with Zomato and its alleged trade practices.[24]

With interest in food and eating out came lifestyle diseases and the relentless focus on fitness. Ten thousand steps a day became a passing fad as innovative fitness regimens came to the forefront. Sugar became the new villain while oil and *ghee* made a stunning comeback to our daily diets.

The nature of shopping changed along lines of festivals. Similar to China, where the singles day rings in billions in sales, the Flipkart Big Billion sale and the Amazon sale were events we looked forward to and we preferred to buy during that period to rake in the massive offers. The biggest success story of us buying goods online was the rise of consumer electronics and in particular mobile phones. With rising consumerism in the economy, we decided to buy high-priced items like mobile phones online with the advent of online only deals, a great range and rise in a minimum threshold of consumers buying online. As a result, e-commerce contributed about 40 per cent of consumer electronics sales.[25]

The holy grail of any Indian household, education and pharmaceuticals, is going online next. In any Indian household, the children's education is given the utmost priority. This was earlier dominated with local tuition providers who raked in a phenomenal amount of money. This category seems to be going online with the rise in Byju's which aims to drive scale and operational profits in the next few years. The real holy grail in India is actually the cash transactions at around 85–90 per cent of the economy. With demonetization and the lure of payment apps, some of us decided to try payments online based on the BHIM app. A fraction of us even decided to buy mutual funds online.

The way we looked at entertainment changed. Most of us stopped watching television for a long period of time. We watched cricket on Hotstar and the hit web series (*Game of thrones*, *Sacred Games*, *Breaking Bad*) on OTT (over-the-top) platforms. This rise of OTT platforms was derived by the utilization of our idle time during our long cab rides on Uber and Ola and the quality of content with the added benefit of convenience. We forgot to use torrents for movies and pirated MP3 songs online as affordability and quality drove out piracy.

In addition, some of us loved to imitate our favourite movie stars on TikTok (its subscriber base was 20 Crores in India and some of them make cringeworthy videos)[26] while the rest of us decided to make our neighbours envious of our lifestyle on Instagram (subscriber base of 8 Crores in India).

The second half of the previous decade was driven in bringing *Bharat online*. While every major player fought over the first 10 Crore consumers based in the Top 10 metros, the real challenge to scale up was to target the next 40 Crore consumers in the next 80–100 cities. Enter the rise of regional content in news (e.g., Dailymotion) and entertainment and local cuisines.

At work, starting your own firm and building your own unicorn started becoming cool. The neighbourhood aunty no longer passed cheap comments at a wannabe entrepreneur as she was amazed at the potential supernormal returns that might be generated due to this successful and unsuccessful journey. Our ecosystem, including entrepreneurship cells at undergraduate colleges and incubator cells at business schools (e.g., NSRCEL in IIM Bangalore), provided necessary guidance for this journey. It was easy to start your own company, from securing finance (if you had the three magical letters of IIT or IIM), utilizing the 'pay per use' technology infrastructure by leveraging SaaS.

At work, there were a million tools that came from start-up companies to make your lives easier. From automated expense filing to smart capability building modules to tools assisting in measuring productivity in sales and spends, entrepreneurs tried to simplify our corporate lives or may be ended up making them more complex.

The next decade will be driven by the need for sound mental health, physical fitness and the return to the benefits of the decades gone by.

Although popular parlance is dominated by the need for more technology-based solutions with jargons of artificial intelligence, neural networks, cyber security and machine learning floating around, the real business ideas lay in key consumer trends likely to emerge in the next decade. Some of these trends include the rise in need for mental health services, targeting specific consumer niches (e.g., young moms, senior citizens, private lives of married couples), need for specific diets (e.g., fat and protein rich, zero carbs) as lifestyle fitness becomes the number one priority. To address the mental health and lifestyle diseases calamity, an associated ecosystem of counsellors and dieticians is likely to rise disproportionately.

As history has shown, humanity keeps moving forward in a decade and decides to go back in the next decade. The offline store is making and will make a stunning comeback in the years to come with the physical presence of touch and feel being valued by consumers. Leading e-commerce players like Xiaomi, Lenskart are already building offline stores. This will be accentuated by the need for lifestyles our grandparents were brought up with, namely, lots of sports grounds and academies and need for physical fitness.

119

While digital was a fashionable word in the previous decade, it might end up being a villain in the next one. There should be a rise in digital detox centres where they consciously jam your phone signals so that you can speak face to face with other human beings. Like China, with rising loneliness and inability of people to communicate face to face, companionship is bound to emerge as a 'pay per use' model.

It is only but natural that leading e-commerce companies will target the holy grail of any FMCG company, the rural Indian consumer. It is interesting to see how this theme will play out. While rural India brings in numbers (35–40% of FMCG sales),[27] it has a higher cost of service of 5–7 per cent of revenue. With none of the unicorns likely to turn operationally profitable soon, the rural theme might actually not play out so well.

The usual suspects will make a fuss about the usual products. There will be hooplas of analytics to drive micromarket efficiencies and newer productivity tools that will measure how you are spending and earning money as a corporate. In a stunning turn of events, 'gut-based decision-making' might make a comeback as excessive data often throws up pictures that are confusing and ends up wasting more time than creating value. As stories capture the human imagination, everyone including you and I is bound to turn a storyteller. Qualitative anecdotes will dominate corporate decision-making rather than the lure of analysis paralysis of hard numbers.

Last but not the least, I think the most important trend will be that consumers will buy and use apps and services that protect their data. Any firm that hints at messing up personal consumer data will go bankrupt overnight.

In conclusion, the next decade promises to be a fun-filled one. It will be interesting to reflect on these predictions when a refresher chapter is written at the end of this decade.

YOUR OFFICE

BRAVING THE WILDERNESS OF CORPORATE INDIA

Your workplace will end up being the single biggest source of joy and misery for you as you will end up spending a majority of your working lives in that space. While a great working culture can lead to higher individual contentment in life, a miserable working culture can make daily corporate routine a painful chore. This section, in a lighter vain, covers the various aspects of corporate work life and culture in India you are bound to face.

Everybody brings joy to this office, some when they enter, some when they exit.
Unknown

Do not underestimate your abilities, that is your boss' job.
Unknown

25

THE FEKU (THE PERENNIAL BLUFF MASTER)

Raghavan, a senior professional, seems to be successful at work but poke a level down—there seems to be distrust in his team with consistent underperformance, stress and a deep sense of misery at his place of work. However, his bosses absolutely love him. Welcome to the age of the Corporate Feku.[28]

It is never easy to work with someone who is always building a narrative, either to hide his underperformance or put someone down or to overcome a deep sense of personality complex. The associated stress, shame, guilt and general misery can be overwhelming for most people. However, such people tend to be successful at their place of work. They are blessed with deep political acumen along with the right blend of sociopathic and narcissistic attributes. Following are some key traits of the Corporate *Feku.*

Always Builds a Narrative, Often a Fake One

The *Corporate Feku* barely performs on most business metrics. However, what they are good at is elevating their role and positioning it as something very big. They will often associate their roles with words including *radical, industry defining, path breaking, transformative, undoing years of poor work.* In addition, before every critical board meeting, they are capable of building a fake narrative of a beautiful future to take people's attention away from the existing gloom and doom.

Always Creates the Right Impression

In addition to building a fake narrative, a tactic that is often employed by the *Corporate Feku* is to carefully manage his own impression. The age-old adage of coming five minutes before your boss and leaving five minutes after your boss is carefully implemented. In addition, there is a conscious display of rigour when very senior professionals are involved. When his bosses are around, the day starts at 7 AM and goes well until midnight. When nobody seems to be around, Pooja Hegde's pictures on Instagram are consciously devoured over.

No Respect for Diversity

The *Corporate Feku* will drive to ascertain domination in the area of thought leadership. Whatever idea or efficiency improvement his team or his peers might come up with, he will always retort with a '*I had already thought of it earlier*'. It is an altogether different problem that very little seems to have been done by him to take care of that idea. An associated corollary employed by the *Corporate Feku* is the lack of respect for women. Although they will proclaim themselves to be champions of gender diversity, they will often pass snide comments about their make-up, facial expressions, lack of seriousness, dressing sense, waistlines.

Psychologically Manipulates His Team Every Day

The *Corporate Feku*, blessed with a high emotional quotient and sociopathic skills, is immensely competent at manipulating his people to work for him without question. A combination of shaming, humiliation, putting people down along with an occasional praise is generously employed to make his people always seek validation for themselves. The classical behavioural psychology that is often employed is the Stockholm syndrome, where the victim tends to sympathize and cheer on his/her perpetrator. One of the most common ways to shame people is to ask them to do a job which is 2–3 levels below their hired level. Another way to drive requisite behaviour is to reward people who blindly support you even if they are underperformers.

No Respect for Anybody's Personal Life

A narrative that elevates the *Corporate Feku's* job is built on making his team work brutal hours. Most of the *Corporate Feku's* team would be working very long hours with limited personal downtime. Such a conscious creation of work and never-ending reviews is carefully crafted to create a perception of industry defining work to everybody else. The focus is often on quantity of work rather than an element of quality or efficiency. In case of any grievance aired, the retort is immediate, *'when I was your age, I would only work and do nothing else.'*

Creates Interpersonal Tension in His Team

The way to build incredible loyalty among disgruntled emotionally manipulated workers is to create interpersonal tension within them. In case a direct subordinate doesn't agree to your targets allocated, call up the subordinate's sub-ordinate and get him to say yes. Then force the subordinate to agree and give him feedback on his people management skills that people under him are extremely unhappy and have complained against him. An additional way is to say something controversial about a team member in someone else's presence and if he diplomatically avoids it, consciously play that comment in that teammate's name on other public forums.

In behavioural psychology, such animalistic behaviour stems from deep-rooted inferiority complex, either due to a lack of formal education or a ghastly firing from the previous job. The ruckus at work is carefully crafted as a conscious display of power. This behaviour can go on for decades without any check or balance. It is difficult for companies to diagnose or counsel such behaviour especially in countries like India where upward feedback is largely symbolic. However, the best course of action for any company is to relieve such characters once they have been suspected of such behaviour. In case you are stuck working with someone who resembles the above character sketch, may God bless you.

The Corporate *Feku* is singlehandedly responsible to build a work culture which is bland at best and toxic at worst. We limit the toxin and look at a sarcastic take on our work culture as part of the next chapter.

26 | OUR FAMED WORK CULTURE

Over the last few years, there have been a few news stories going viral.[29] In France, employees are heavily discouraged to mail or read emails after 6 PM This is in addition to their 35-hour work week. Germany has gone one step ahead and is considering banning communication after work hours. Research conducted among nurses in Sweden indicates that a six-hour working day boosts productivity and leads to greater personal satisfaction. The practice is being extended to other private firms in Sweden (e.g., Toyota Service Center).[30] It is not coincidental that such friendly behaviour emerges in European countries. In fact, I once read a research article that suggested the best countries to work in were in Europe or Australia. The bottom three in that list—China, South Korea and India—didn't come as a surprise. While the 'Indian way' of working has been acclaimed the world over for its aptitude, planning and robust execution, there are certain characteristics that define us as a race. Well, it is applicable to most of us if not all of us.

We Love Each Other's Faces

Our love for 'Facetime', for our colleague's and junior's faces is legendary. Given that we come from the land where mythological characters have multiple faces, our love for each other's faces is understandable. Instead of the popular adage that 'time is money', the popular adage for our times is 'facetime is money'. It stems from our deep-rooted desire to be a part of a larger community and always be in the company of each other. The longer a guy stays in office, the more delayed into the night his email is, the more late night his flight on a Friday is, the more respected he is. One of my batchmates once described his supervisor of relapsing into a fit of 'part convulsion, part constipation' when he suggested to him that he had finished all his work by 6 PM and wanted to go home. After all, unless your face burns the midnight oil, there is little merit in moving upward.

Let's Get the Desi Flavour in

If you have noticed any sitcoms on television, the Indian character is always shown in a certain way. Doesn't take vacations. Sits till late every day. Does nothing on Friday evening. Overweight. No physical activity—running, jogging or playing a game. While such a caricature might be funny to Western audiences, we take pride in our emerging belly as everybody likes to be associated with a *khaata-peeta-ghar* tag. In fact, a research quoted by the *New Straits Times* suggested that Indian service employees are the most obese amongst all races. While others might cringe at the prospect of being the most overweight race, we clearly don't. The same batchmate, I alluded to earlier, referred to the convulsions of his supervisor when he realized that my batchmate would go running every morning. His supervisor's argument was simple, why can't he use that one hour to deliver more output at work?

We Love Mahendra Singh Dhoni and His Approach of Taking Everything to the End

Have you ever wondered why we always have a late night before a key meeting or a workshop? Why everything seems to change or be done in the last minute? The answer is very simple, it comes from our deep-rooted admiration for Mahendra Singh Dhoni. MS Dhoni's success by having taken matches to the last over and delivering in most cases has left an indelible mark on our psyche. So we continue our childhood obsession of putting in a late night before the exams to our professional lives.

Let's Go Completely Hardcore and Create 'xxx' Value

It is deep rooted in our society to deliver a little more than what is asked for. If your boss asks for 'x', we push our juniors to go hardcore and deliver 'xxx'. It is after all a larger philosophy to be office centric and stretch more and more. Hence, our oft expressed attribute to create work 24×7. In the name of 'excellence', we always ask some questions to push everybody to find their inner calling. Can we add more sources? Can we do this better? Should we go into the next level of detail? Why don't we do this too?

We Love to Complicate Working Conditions

The Google campus is famous for many things—Google Pod to take a quick nap, showers, gyms and so on. But they are not really relevant for our race. Although a lot of Indian offices offer such things, but who wants to take these up. It is criminal to go to the gym to waste time and be healthy. We would rather sit in our cubicles and pile on the kilos instead. And we abhor the concept of 'work from home'. It is spiritually draining to miss out on the office atmosphere. It is an extension of our earlier principle of our undisputed love for each other's faces.

In conclusion, there is nothing else to be said. We are like this only. Well, almost across the board. If it wasn't, you wouldn't have been reading till here. If you can't bear this toxin any longer, there are innovative ways to say bye. Read on as part of the next chapter.

27

GREAT WAYS TO EXIT YOUR CURRENT BOSS

In the services industry, moving in and out of assignments is everyday stuff. However, even service industry professionals get stuck on projects with horrendous bosses who refuse to let go off them. However, these consultants come up with remarkable excuses to rid themselves of the horror of their bosses or horrible project locations. The following excuses are all real and can be used by you too in your day-to-day work.[31]

Like with most things in life, I will divide the excuses under four broad buckets—personality driven excuses, biological driven excuses, radical excuses and miscellaneous excuses. *(I should assure you that all of the following anecdotes are based on real characters. You can look up my contacts list on social media and start guessing who they might be.)*

Personality-Driven Excuses: Hollywood Calling

Ms Bareja, a hot shot MBA from IIM Calcutta, was one of the smartest women I had worked with. She decided to roll off her current client, a government electricity company, as she wasn't getting enough intellectual kick from her work. When the project manager refused to let go of her, she decided to give the mighty Cameron Diaz multiple sleepless nights.

At every lunch conversation, she would only file nails instead of talking about quality intellectual business insights. Whenever the manager asked her to do something, she would look blank at him like she was going to pass out. Out of nowhere, she would start pointing to a person and start laughing raucously at him. Although she managed to exit, she was tagged with some baggage—names like 'aspirational dumb blonde', 'preliminary psycho' being a couple of them.

Biological-Driven Excuses: Right Out of 'Sex and the City'

One of the most glamorous colleagues, an ex-Ms Chandigarh, I worked with got staffed on a project completely against her choice in Northeast India, specifically the India–China border. She didn't seem to fall short on innovative thinking on each day of the week.

On every Monday: 'I have stomach cramps. I won't be coming to the India–China border today. Somebody will have to do my work.'

On every Wednesday: 'I am having a bad hair day', 'I have a bad stomach', 'I want to puke'. My manager, a *TamBram* (Tamil Brahmin) from a middle-class family, was taught to be extremely polite to a woman's needs. As a result, he would give her Wednesday off.

On every Friday: 'I am feeling very weak. I think I have iron deficiency.' She started contracting iron deficiency on Friday afternoon due to her excessive drinking on Thursday night.

Finally, when the manager was still not relieving her from the project, she came up with, 'I have severe neck ache. My doctor has advised me complete bed rest for the next three weeks. I cannot sit straight for more than 15 minutes'. She was finally relieved from the project.

Later that weekend, both my manager and her happened to visit Blue Frog Club in Mumbai where she was spotted viciously shaking her pelvis to *Babli Badmaash*. Ouch.

Radical Excuses: Adam and Eve Would Be So Proud of This

Rahul Sampath, from IIM Ahmedabad, was staffed on a project that operated out of the Namibia border. Our HR team had convinced him to take up the project by branding him as the head of our Namibian operations. Once reality sank in, the Namibian border fell marginally short of resembling Manhattan in New York, he tried to desperately roll off but the account lead wouldn't let him.

He tried to reason with the lead on how he was suffering in the border area but met with limited success. He managed to produce fake medical certificates of vitamin deficiency, iron deficiency, scabies, allergies to various Namibian plants, yellow and brown fever. The account lead refused to relent an inch.

As a last resort, he managed to get his wife pregnant from Namibia. The account lead didn't have a choice but to let him go so that he could stay close to his 'expecting' wife.

Miscellaneous Excuses: 'Beat It'—Michael Jackson Style!

In true corporate India style, everything that cannot be straight jacketed into any bucket is always clubbed under 'Miscellaneous Excuses'. The best one I have heard till date is, 'I have to go for dance practice every day at 5 PM A choreographer is coming to train me over the next six months. I need to impress my wife's family at my Sangeet'. His supervisor rolled him off with immediate effect.

In conclusion, no matter how torturous your stint has been, it is foolish to mess up your relationship with your client or your current team members. It is advisable to wrap up your work and do a good job at handing over your responsibility to your successor. Finally, in the services industry, performance metrics are largely subjective, it rarely helps to piss off someone senior in the hierarchy. In all likelihood, you will come across him or her in the future.

28

APPEARING SMART IN MEETINGS WITHOUT HAVING ANY CLUE

In modern-day jobs, corporate meetings tend to fill up a ridiculous portion of our lives. An average person tends to spend five to six hours every day attending meetings. Given this barrage of meetings we all attend, it is difficult to be prepared and participate wholeheartedly in all of them. The following guide is a useful primer to appear smart in meetings when you have no clue. Absolutely no clue.[32]

Ask Leadership-Type Questions

In our society, leadership is often touted as the solution to all of mankind's problems. Given this background, you should always consider asking leadership-type questions to appear smart in a meeting. The following questions always hold irrespective of whether you are attending a meeting to remove lizards in the office building or double your company's sales, 'Can we do this faster? Can we do this better? Can we do this in a structured manner? Can we make this tighter? Can we come up with a more innovative solution?'

Act Like Leadership

The rule mentioned above is a starting point to appear smart. The real deal is to act like a true leader. If you have no clue about what is happening in a meeting, it is advisable to walk up to the white board and start writing random points about what people in the room are talking about. People love leaders who lead from the front. In addition, if you are able to draw a Venn diagram to depict the same points, you will be up for CEO of the year.

Use Intelligent Phrases

If the meeting is high on content and you have not been able to contribute to the discussion yet, an easy lifeline the world has granted you is to make use of intelligent phrases. When in trouble, reiterate the following phrases in an iterative tantric chant, *'Let us take a step back. What is the big picture here? Can we put our hands on our heart and proclaim that this is in our company's best interest? Are we really being strategic here? How do we scale up?'* In addition, if you have done theatre in your life, it is advisable to get up at this point and start strolling around in the room with the gravitas of Don Corleone in *The Godfather*.

Help People Maximize Their Washroom Potential

Meetings in India run long, very long. In such a scenario, you can easily endear to the other participants by managing logistics in the meeting. Try taking the ownership of the AC remote. Increase the temperature and then decrease it every 10 minutes. Ask the office boy to bring in tea and biscuits every 15 minutes. Look awkwardly at one person in the room repeatedly and ask if he needs to use the washroom now.

Appear to Be Funny

After some time, meetings can become very dry and boring. Another aspect of leadership is to engage the participants in the room by making them laugh. Start narrating Santa Banta jokes or get everyone to ogle at the latest pictures of an emerging movie starlet. Instagram is a great place to get started to source pictures of various movie starlets. In no time, you will be appointed as the Chief Entertainment Officer.

Support a Colleague

Corporate jobs are about supporting colleagues and getting them to fulfil their potential. Hence in a meeting, it is of utmost importance to make them feel special. Repeat what a colleague has said—slowly, very slowly, with gravitas. If possible, punching the table too will help. Your colleague will be grateful for this gesture all through her life.

Think Deep, Very Deep

It is important to emerge as a thought leader in a critical meeting. As a result, start taking down notes voraciously. It is important to appear to be taking down notes even if you are actually writing down your weekend binge watching list on Netflix. However, to avoid appearing like the secretary in the room, it is advisable to stop taking down notes midway and to glare at the person speaking for a few minutes and then nod in agreement after some time.

Gadgets Matter, Duh!

There is a reason Steve Jobs charged such a high premium for all the beautiful gadgets he made. Carrying one of his fancy gadgets often lends an air of creditability and respect to the person attending the meeting. It is a rewarding investment to buy an iPad to take notes. You can use your iPad to take notes and draw cartoons of your boss simultaneously.

Get Lots and Lots of Printouts

This rule works in conjunction with the previous rule. Although you might have an iPad to take notes, it is still advisable to carry a printout of a 100-page document. It doesn't matter if the document is the script of *Fifty Shades of Grey* where you have highlighted the provocative portions. Carrying such documents automatically lifts the stature of an individual in a meeting. It is advisable to pretend to refer to page #42 in the middle of the meeting and then nod in agreement with everyone.

The Oldest Rule in the Book, Use Jargons

The true test of a leader is to sound intelligent in a room. The world has devised specific resources on the internet where you can generously lift jargons to appear intelligent. The biggest source of intelligent management jargon is on *random bullshit generator (dot) com* where you get a dosage into the latest jargons being employed the world over. Some of the bestselling phrases are '*matrix customized partnerships, enhance seamless e-markets, cultivate distributed applications, synergize front end mindshare and so on*'.

In conclusion, it is not easy making a career in corporate India. Succeeding in corporate meetings are a critical element in building a personal brand and driving individual success. The above primer should go a long way in generating corporate success.

WATER COOLER TALK

THE MODERN-DAY WORLD TRENDS

There are many contemporary topics of discussion you are expected to know and speak on, at the water cooler in office, to impress your division head or to sound cool in front of the new good-looking intern. Unfortunately, these topics are never covered in any business textbook. I have curated close to a dozen such topics which you should be knowing to appear as a smart millennial. I should clarify I am not saying you are not smart already.

October - this is one of the particularly dangerous months to invest in stocks. Other dangerous months are July, January, September, April, November, May, March, June, December, August and February.
Mark Twain

Success and failure are both difficult to endure. Along with success come drugs, divorce, bullying, travel, meditation, medication, depression, neurosis and suicide. With failure comes failure.
Joseph Heller
author of the book *Catch-22*

29

GREATEST FINANCIAL CRISES OVER THE LAST FEW DECADES

The world has seen many an asset bubble inflate and go bust over the last few decades. Some of these crashes have had devastating consequences on the economy, employment, consumer sentiment and country GDP. Although these crises have happened across decades, their underlying principles seem eerily similar—a speculation bubble leading to a massive increase in asset prices (e.g., real estate, stock markets) followed by a panic sell off and a huge drop in consumer sentiment and eventual resurrection of the economy led by easing monetary policy of the government and tapering of adverse consumer sentiment. This primer looks at some of the biggest crises in the last few decades which everyone should be aware of.

The Great Economic Depression of 1929-1939[33]

The Great Depression is by far the worst economic crisis of the 20th century led by the United States and eventually to the other developed nations. The crisis lasted a decade resulting in severe job losses, record unemployment hitting 25 per cent at its worst and the American GDP falling by over 30 per cent.

The genesis of the crisis was the crash of the American stock markets in 1929, dipping 29 per cent over a short period of time, initiating on a day also termed as Black Thursday, as investors started panic selling having lost faith in the strength of the American economy. This economic crash was preceded by a booming stock market that rose four times from 1921 to 1927 on the back of easy money availability. The central bank, in an attempt to control asset prices, raised interest rates. This led to a depression in consumption in sectors like construction and auto which were heavily dependent on easy availability of credit. A panic on the stock markets further jolted consumer sentiment as purchase of consumer durables were delayed further dampening an economic recovery. As consumers wanted to liquidate their deposits stored in banks, the banks had reduced capital to loan out further reducing money supply in the system and creating a vicious negative spiral. The recovery of the economy was eventually initiated after the government eased monetary policy and devalued the US dollar along with abandoning the gold standard.

Is That So?

1. Did you know that famous Chicago gangster Al Capone opened a soup kitchen during the Great Depression? For millions, soup kitchens provided the only food they would see all day.

The Crash of the Tiger Economies[34]

The 90s saw the booming rise of the Southeast Asian tiger economies (Malaysia, Philippines, Indonesia, Singapore and Thailand) on the back of exports and liberalization of their economies. This liberalization led to massive foreign capital flowing into these countries as they started reporting impressive growth in GDP. This period of boom led to real estate prices which were artificially high. As its relative attractiveness reduced once the United States increased interest rates and real estate prices became untenable, foreign capital shifted away from these tiger economies. This led to an economic crash starting with the Thai government abandoning its fixed currency pegging to the US dollar citing inadequate foreign exchange resources and devaluing the Thai baht as a result. As other tiger economies also started devaluing their currencies, there was a wave of inflation, as foreign goods and commodities like oil were more expensive, leading to other problems for the economy. At its worst, the stock markets in these regions nearly lost 50 per cent of their value from their peak. The tiger economies started recovering again in 1999 after the International Monetary Fund intervened with a short-term loan of $100 billion to Thailand, Indonesia and South Korea. In return, these economies were supposed to increase interest rates, privatize state-owned companies, reduce public spending and raise taxes. The tiger economies since then have consistently emerged as the fastest-growing countries across the world.

Is That So?

1. Did you know that hedge fund manager, George Soros, made a massive bet in excess of a billion dollars against the Thai Baht during 1997, before the impending tiger economies crisis? After the crash, many Southeast Asian political leaders including the Malaysian Prime Minister attacked George Soros for unnecessarily attacking Southeast Asian currencies.

The Big Dot Com Crash in 1998-2000[35]

Also referred to as the internet bubble, the dot com crash in the last 90s (while some of you were in your nappies) was initiated due to the relentless flow of easy money into internet-oriented companies that had limited revenues and profits to show for. The investors had an inherent belief that these companies would generate insane revenue and profits in course of time, but these expectations came to a halting grind. The American stock market, the NASDAQ, rose five times between 1995 and 2000 and fell 76 per cent from 2000 to 2002 to eventually go back to the 1995 levels. During this blind phase of investing, investors ignored traditional metrics to evaluate companies like revenue growth, profitability, price/earning per share (PE ratio) while they put in their investments blindly behind these companies. However, some technology companies that started during that phase still continue to flourish, Google and Amazon being prime examples.

Is That So?

1. Did you know that, webvan.com, an online grocery delivery service, saw its valuation plummet from $1.2 bn to almost nothing during the dot com crash?
2. Did you know that during the dot com crash, Cisco lost 86 per cent of its market capitalization while Amazon saw its share price crashing from 107$ to 10$?

The Sub-prime Crisis of 2007[36]

The sub-prime crisis of 2007 has been the biggest economic crisis of the 21st century with most of us having witnessed it first hand. The crisis was led by the collapse of the housing bubble in 2007–2008 in the United States with home loan buyers starting to default collectively on their mortgage payments. The crisis was actually initiated five years ago, when the central bank started easing monetary supply after the dot com crash and the 9/11 terrorist attacks. With easy money available, many financial institutions lent money to consumers with poor credit records so that they could buy their dream homes. The initial mortgage payment was very low and interest rates would slowly increase as the loan tenure kept moving forward. As the interest payments rose, many of these low creditworthy consumers couldn't pay for their loans leading to a collective collapse in real estate prices. This triggered a crisis in financial agencies like Wall Street banks with players like Lehman brothers eventually going bankrupt. In addition, investment banks collectively sold these loans, also termed as mortgage-backed securities, to other investors on the back of a promise that in a large pool only a few of them would default. As there was a collective failure of interest payments, other investors took a hammering in their holdings triggering a global crisis. The crisis exposed the soft underbelly of the US financial markets with credit agencies struggling to flag off risk in poor quality investments, misaligned incentives of banks issuing loans to poor creditworthy consumers and the lack of control of the regulator to prevent such untoward moves. The global economy has taken nearly five years to recover from the aftermath of the sub-prime crisis on the back of a bailout package designed by the US government and significant easing of money supply.

Is That So?

1. Did you know that the movie The Big Short, comprising of Christian Bale and Brad Pitt, is based on the 2007 sub-prime crisis in the United States?

The 1991 Economic Crisis in India[37]

Back home, the 1991 economic crisis is one of the most landmark moments resulting in the development of the

Indian economy. The Indian economy struggled in the late 1980s with a high balance of payments as exports shrunk with India's major partner, Russia (then USSR) imploding and import bills, primarily oil, rising with the Gulf war. As India was left with only three weeks of reserves to fund imports, it embarked on a journey of liberalization as it was one of the conditions of the World Bank to lend it a short-term loan.

As part of the journey, India opened its economy to international players, slashed import duties and licensing, removed production licenses and promised to cut red tape. It strived to encourage foreign investors and showed an inclination to privatize inefficient government-owned companies. The huge population was given access to the global markets which has eventually led to nearly three decades of prosperous and high single-digit growth.

Is That So?

1. In the 1991 crisis in India, did you know that the government had to pledge its physical gold to the World Bank for an interim short-term loan to overcome its payments crisis?

In conclusion, all the great disasters across global economies over the last century have seemed eerily similar. It is led on the back of easy money supply that leads to artificial asset price increases (e.g., real estate, stock markets). Once investors realize that their optimism about the economy is misplaced, there is panic selling leading to a stock market crash, a slowdown in consumer sentiment and declining GDP. Eventually, the government intervenes on the back of easy monetary supply and incentives to drive the economy back again.

30   OVERCOMING THE DEMAND SLOWDOWN*

The popular business press is filled with stories of a slowing economy (as of end 2019), expected to hover around mid-single digits. The reason for this slowdown has been attributed to slowing consumption, which accounts for over 50 per cent of our GDP. Across sectors like auto, FMCG and consumer durables, this slowdown is visible with differing levels of intensity. The stinging part of this slowdown has been rural India which has been growing at 1.5 times urban India growth over the last three to five years. This is primarily due to lack of available credit, limited disposable income due to minimum support prices which are not increasing at the same proportional rate and inadequate jobs. While the government is expected to and is taking measures to tide over this slowdown, leading consumption-oriented companies are looking at the following themes to beat the consumption blues.[38]

Easy Financing of Your Trade Partners

As consumers are delaying purchases, especially non-disposable ones, distributors are facing a liquidity crunch as they have huge piles of inventory as companies have billed their goods but consumers are not buying from retailers, and hence they are not getting cashback from the retailers to fund their inventory. As a result, leading auto and FMCG

---

* The thoughts and solution themes mentioned in this chapter are based on my discussions with various industry leaders in FMCG.

companies are looking at different ways to support their distributors. While a company like Maruti Suzuki is embarking on centralized negotiations with third-party financiers so that their distributors get 1 to 1.5 per cent better rates on borrowing money, Jockey has extended its credit period to its distributors to support them during this slowdown. It is also to be noted that while some distributors have adequate capital to keep investing in their business, after GST implementation, they are hesitating and rightfully so, to keep their unaccounted money in their distribution business.

Single Consumption Packs to Lure the Rural Consumer In

Given rural comprises about 40 per cent of FMCG sales and is primarily hit with the consumption slowdown, leading FMCG companies are using their age-old maxim to churn out smaller packs to attract consumers to shift from unorganized to branded players. There are ₹1 chocolate slabs, single use masala packs, Nestlé pushing its mini Maggi (35 grams) pack and single use perfume packs that are being deployed extensively. It is one of the reasons why most of the leading FMCGs have still been reporting mid to high single digit growth rates.

Spend and Scream Your Lungs Away

To keep the rural consumer invested in, leading FMCGs are continuing to invest in rural-oriented activations, namely, village *haats*, wall paintings, local hoardings and communication over local media. The underlying principle is that most leading companies are not willing to compromise on top-line growth but are more acceptable to a 0.5 to 1 per cent reduction in EBITDA margins due to the higher investment on a smaller base.

Lower the Play on Premiumization unless It Is Super Premium

Over the last few years, leading consumption companies have embarked on the premiumization journey to cater to the aspiring middle classes and increasing their profit margins as a result.

While there have been news of Hector MG selling out its premium launch models or iPhone 11 Pro series selling out in five days from its launch, companies are slowing down on the premiumization route unless it is a super-premium model route. For instance, Maruti Suzuki is going back to what it does best, making a value for money vehicle in the form of its mini SUV S-Presso. This behaviour is based on the principle that revenue from premium models constitute 12–15 per cent of business while rural constitutes about 40 per cent of business and is the future of growth as the next 200 million consumers will come from there.

Return of the Offline Consumer

While e-commerce and omni-channel experience have been the words of the year for the last few years, the likely trend in the next few years is going to be the re-emergence of the offline channel. E-commerce growths are reducing (to 20%) as there is a decline in deep discounting, offline channels matching online prices and an increasing perception on the poorer quality of goods (especially apparel) being sold online. As a result, there is an increasing trend of leading consumption companies setting up offline channels like One

Plus, Xiaomi, Realme along with Amazon selling its private labels in 2100 stores in Future Group, More and Shoppers Stop. As consumers slowly prefer the offline channel again (e-commerce has very little channel penetration at 3–6% anyway), the real battle will move to winning each physical outlet over.

Supply Side Efficiency and Passing the Benefit on to Consumers

As raw material input commodity prices soften the world over (e.g., prices of input material copra are down by 20% assisting Parachute), the resultant benefit in cost inputs are being passed onto consumers of economy products. For instance, Unilever reduced its prices in Lifebuoy by 5 per cent (up to 20% in certain products) to lure the price discerning consumer to make them shift from unorganized players to branded players. This trend is likely to continue in industries which have a significant channel exposure to rural India. In addition, efficiency in supply chain mechanics is also likely to be passed onto the price discerning consumer going forward.

Drive Alternate Channels of Revenue

Given the domestic slowdown, the exports market is likely to emerge as an important channel of focus. With a consistently depreciating rupee and South East and Middle East Asian countries doing relatively well, leading consumption players are likely to drive exports to these shores to build an additional buffer. Simultaneously, Modern Trade, from an existing channel contribution of ~10 per cent, is likely to be focussed on (e.g., GCPL, Marico), as the consumer likely to purchase a larger assortment or premium packs is likely to visit there. Needless to say, ambitious market entries in newer categories are expected to be put on the back burner till consumer confidence numbers move in the right direction.

In conclusion, the consumption slowdown is expected to continue for the next few quarters. As leading consumption companies implement the above principles, it is only a matter of time to see who laugh their way to the financial markets and who pant away to plummeting finances.

31

NEED TO DO EVERYTHING

One of the bedrocks in strategy exercises the world over was to be consistent and drive focus—in positioning, execution or communication. It has always been taught and practised that delving in too many things is suboptimal. It has been consistently advised to have a clear position. However, with changing times, this oft-practised philosophy is being revisited as consumer-oriented businesses try to simultaneously delve across multiple ends of the same spectrum. This chapter looks at key dimensions in front-end consumer facing businesses.[39]

To Be or Not to Be

One of the sharpest changes that has occurred is in operating philosophies of consumer-oriented businesses. A decade ago, the key question for consumer companies, especially technology start-ups, was to choose between being a *big fish in a small pond* (think PayPal in early 2000s) or a *small fish in a big pond* (think Dell when it started). In contemporary times, the operating philosophy is often to strive to be the *biggest fish in the biggest pond* (think of the new age technology giants in Silicon Valley).

My Channel or Yours

It is extremely interesting to see how consumer-oriented businesses address the channel issue. They often adopt a simultaneous contradictory strategy of 'channel control' (think Xiaomi having its own stores to establish channel control) and 'channel outsource' (think Xiaomi driving more than a third of its sales from online channels where it has little control). In addition, the quality of distribution also seems to be suffering from this contradictory focus. Leading FMCGs are adopting a contradictory strategy of adopting both 'high quality distribution' (think direct distribution) and 'low quality distribution' (think indirect distribution via wholesale) with equal fervour.[40]

To control the channel is good, so is to outsource the channel. To pursue direct distribution is good. Equally good is to pursue indirect distribution.

Fifteen Minds within a Mind

Leading consumer-oriented businesses adopt a strategy of 'one size fits all' (think all strategy exercises done at the beginning of the year talking about one consistent consumer proposition) and 'multiple sizes for multiple people' (think Unilever having more than a dozen mini Indias) while defining their consumer profiles. Both these seemingly contradictory philosophies seem to be happily married.

Schrodinger's Manpower—On and Off My Payroll at the Same Time

Treatment of frontline manpower is akin to a newly married couple. They start off by being very close (think front line manpower on a company's payroll) and slowly drift apart (think front line manpower being outsourced to a third-party agency). Depending on the ebbs and flows in a couple's relationship, leading FMCGs keep absorbing manpower on their payroll and then outsourcing them to a third-party agency. However, at any point of time, front line manpower often stays 'on and off' a company's payroll.

Be Like a Bottle of Wine—Marry the Appeal of the Old to the New

Almost every consumer durable firm's operating strategy is to penetrate the old (think rural) and the new (think e-commerce) at the same time. Rural and e-commerce operate at two ends of the spectrum targeting different age groups, regions, buyer values and relative affluence. The structure and executional capability required to tap into both of them are vastly different. However, most of these consumer-facing businesses seem to be running after both of them at the same time.

Key Focus Product Is Every Product

Product portfolio strategies of most consumer facing product companies are borderline hilarious. They typically range along the following diktats. Every new product is focus. Every old product is focus. Every core product is focus. Every non-core product is focus. Every product has potential. Every product is the future. Every product is important. Every product needs to be invested in. Every product needs depth. Every product needs breadth.

You Are a Premium but Basic Player, I Am a Basic but Premium Player

As a result of the product strategies, the pricing propositions of most consumer-oriented businesses (barring Apple) seem eerily similar. A basic company has products from entry level to premium. A premium company has products from entry level to premium.

In conclusion, the explanation for this schizophrenic behaviour is fairly straightforward. With increasing competition and decades of growth, vast barren opportunity appears limited. However, there are pockets of micromarkets that exist for lucrative tapping. To tap into these micromarkets, which are not related and are spread across the spectrum, consumer-oriented businesses need to operate across contradictory elements in the spectrum. Hence, revisiting what has been taught and practised over decades of experience seems inevitable.

Or it is just 'good greed' where everyone wants to play everywhere to capture everything. What is sauce for the goose is also sauce for the gander.

32

THE LURE OF RURAL INDIA*

The single biggest discussion in boardrooms of consumption-oriented companies - FMCG, consumer durables, auto and now financial services, has been the immense opportunity of rural India. For the last few years, rural India has been propped up as a once in a lifetime opportunity that cannot be missed upon. Is the rural bandwagon a hidden diamond or a Trojan horse?[41]

It is a no-brainer to fathom why rural India is getting most businesses excited. Two-thirds of our population stays there across six lakh villages. More and more studies indicate that rural incomes are rising at early double digits, as of 2018, and their consumption is growing faster than urban India. Leading FMCGs have rural contributing close to one third of their top line with Unilever and Dabur generating more than 40 per cent of their top-line from rural India. With 4G connectivity on the rise, thanks to Jio, rural India is getting connected to Urban India at an alarming pace.

However, there are certain challenges that remain with doing business with rural India. The cost to serve for serving rural markets are 7–9 per cent (of revenue) higher than urban markets. In addition, succeeding in rural India depends on activation of strong influencer networks—*sarpanches* for auto, housewives for FMCG, leveraging public centres and community hotspots—all of which are difficult to execute and expensive on-ground activations.

---

* For a more nuanced view into rural India, you may read https://www.nielsen.com/in/en/insights/report/2018/planning-the-route-to-growth-in-rural-markets/

With net profits of most consumer-oriented companies in early double digits, the incremental cost to serve is a hefty price to pay. In addition, the quality of on-ground labour and their persistent attrition puts 10–15 per cent of steady rural business at considerable risk. Moreover, leading companies face tremendous competition from local brands or from counterfeit products. For instance, it can be amusing to see the number of eerily looking similar bottles of Parachute hair oil in rural Andhra Pradesh. The entire business from rural India is dependent on monsoons and crop productivity which is largely out of control of any leading company. All of these make doing business with rural India at best profit neutral. For instance, most branches of PSUs in rural India have not turned profitable. The additional cost to serve for rural India has made the return on capital employed for leading consumer companies significantly lower than the opportunity cost of capital (10%–12%).

So why does everybody get so excited with rural India? For starters, the sheer opportunity size is mind boggling. Moreover, for leading companies that have explored most micromarkets (e.g., metro, tier 1, tier 2), rural is the last untapped opportunity that is an avenue for top-line growth. The underlying assumption is that with scale comes efficiency, which will hopefully translate to profits someday. For companies who are not in the bracket of Unilever, it is a theme that can be delayed for now. For sane-headed companies with limited capital, the better theme to focus might still be premiumization in metro and at best Tier 1 towns. While premiumization can be difficult with competitive pressures in metros, it is a theme that is easier to tap into with the rise of the aspirational booming middle class.

Given that as Indians, we suffer from the *log kya kahenge* syndrome, it is difficult to ignore a theme everyone seems to be obsessing over. So, at best, a limited presence to tap into rural markets might be a good idea. To minimize the burden of cost to serve, it is best to serve the Top 20,000/600,000 villages that provide 60 per cent of the rural opportunity. It is advisable to avoid a direct network and to leverage a partner network, for instance a feeder wholesale to tap into these areas. Needless to say, only a limited selection of SKUs, primarily easy on the wallet and with significant brand strength would operate in these areas.

In conclusion, although rural seems a no-brainer, it is a theme that can be very risky for companies with limited capital. With India expected to see the dual themes of premiumization and rural play out in the next decade, premiumization might seem a better fit for companies who are not blessed with unlimited cash to burn.

Like the lazy Garfield would often say, '*It is sometimes best to do nothing and let someone else figure it out for you!*'

33

MINIMALISM AT WORK

We live in a world where multiple fads rage every few years.[42] From specialist hobbies (read photography) to exotic dance forms (read Zumba) to dietary fascinations (read keto), the 'age of fads' is truly here. The latest fad that seems to be taking over corporates, especially high-end management professionals, seems to be the notion of professional minimalism. This doesn't refer to the minimalist workspace but the entire outlook to a professional career.[43]

Minimalism, as a concept, owes its origin to Buddhism. It is linked to principles of detachment, mindfulness and focus. The philosophy looks down upon rampant materialism which constantly leads to unhappiness. The 'keeping up with the Joneses' syndrome rarely ends up making anyone happy. Minimalism aides in eliminating unnecessary stress and focusing on more productive activities. The application of the philosophy is not new to business, its role in design and development of key Apple products is legendary; so is the design of clutter-free, paper-free workspaces.

Professional minimalism builds on this philosophy in everyday interactions. This is not to be confused with the preachy 'follow your heart' type of speeches which list out five ways to find happiness by quitting your job and doing something you love. Wait till the next EMI of your house in Mumbai reaches your doorstep.

Rather, it starts with minimizing unnecessary discussions. As a guideline, all meetings should forcibly end in an hour, if it doesn't end, another slot should be fixed later on. The first one might be unfruitful but over a period of time, meetings become efficient. All memos, discussion notes should be crafted in one page. More than that implies the sponsor lacks clarity in thought. A lot of energy is often spent on topics not directly related to someone's life. Is it worth passionately fighting with a colleague over which political party is better? Can the time and energy be used on something more productive?

A corollary of the above thought process also involves minimalistic written communication. A lot of us are guilty of typing out long emails with complicated sentences with unnecessary adjectives and adverbs. The philosophy advocates emails to be three to five bullet points long. Any new idea should be explained in one page. Presentations should not have more than five main slides. The human mind takes 30 seconds to implicitly decide 'yes' or 'no' to something. Three to five slides are often good enough to impact that decision. Unfortunately, the number of slides in a presentation is often taken as a proxy for competence and hard work. The golden principle while constructing presentations is simple, will the idea collapse if that slide is not there? Often, it is only three to four slides that stand the principle.

Professional networking is often stressed upon as a key driver for success in modern-day business. The minimalist approach focuses on adding only two to three key contacts per year but investing significant time and effort in them. Over a period of time, it makes sense to have a few solid professional relationships rather than a gamut of low-quality ones. Don't like someone? Just block them on your phone and your social media pages. It is advisable to give no space to unfavourable interactions.

At the cost of repetition, minimalism is the exact opposite of materialism. Common parlance in minimalist theory suggests the number of material possessions should not cross 51. While others say the magic number is 101, the larger point is to be ruthless and limit the number of material possessions.

It is fairly obvious to go easy on the number of gadgets and possessions. If the tablet is not adding any tangible value to your life, it is not required. Same with the fitness band and the music player. It also involves minimizing the number of bank accounts, credit cards, pens and contacts on the phone. There is little pride in flaunting five different credit cards with five different types of benefits. The share of mind space occupied by them is completely unproductive.

From a work perspective, it often involves doing only three to five things every day and leaving the rest. Once the most important things get done every day, work stabilizes automatically. The philosophy of working efficiently and leaving office on time every day goes along with it.

While there are other aspects to building a focused minimalistic mind by limiting unnecessary variations in diet, sleeping patterns and clothing, they are best left for a discussion in another chapter.

In conclusion, the elements mentioned above are rudimentary and can aid to remove clutter and noise in day-to-day business interactions. It can also help in removing the debt trap and driving away the necessary evil of borrowed plastic spending.

However, in certain work contexts, adopting some of these can be tricky if not detrimental to professional success. Only time can answer if this fad stays on or will be replaced by the next one in queue.

34

CHEMICALS IN GOOD LEADERS

Ashish Raman, a modern-day rockstar manager, was famous in his company for setting aggressive deadlines to his team members, stretched targets, promoting healthy competition and constantly pushing his team outside their comfort zone. Working late nights were a norm. He believed in the concept of a hard-working employee who was ambitious, passionate about work and ready to burn the midnight oil.[44]

I recently saw a video on the chemical analysis of leadership by biologist Simon Senek.[45] He advocated that the inherent chemistry of an individual reflected in his leadership. Traditionally, leadership has always been understood and taught through many lenses, behavioural, motivational, personality and so on. There are numerous theories that explain the various styles and facets of leadership. Interestingly, good leaders and good teams show a similar slew of good chemicals while bad leaders and consequently bad teams show a slew of undesirable chemicals. The million-dollar question is—can the chemical mix of a good leader be replicated?

According to his video, there are five key chemicals that define the leadership profile of an individual—Endorphin, Dopamine, Serotonin, Oxytocin and Cortisol.

Endorphin is best known as the masking physical pain chemical. For instance, a runner feels exhilarated after finishing a marathon despite his body being subjected to acute physical stress. The 'runner's high' is primarily due to the release of endorphin. Similarly, endorphin is activated for people in the gymnasium or while undertaking heavy exercises. From a leadership perspective, endorphin is required for the long nights, weekend work and travelling in middle seats in late-night flights.

Dopamine, an extremely addictive 'achievement' chemical, is activated when something has been accomplished. For instance, dopamine is activated when someone meets their sales targets or ticks off an item from their to-do list. It is a classical explanation for sales employees who are constantly driven to achieve their targets, as on each achievement, dopamine, a happy chemical, is released. On the contrary, dopamine being highly addictive is associated with alcoholism, smoking and gambling. From a leadership perspective, setting achievable targets with multiple intermediate steps can set-up many dopamine releasing points for the team.

Serotonin, the leadership chemical, is activated on feeling proud or a feeling of status. Serotonin, unlike Endorphin and Dopamine, is released for both the giver and the receiver. From a leadership perspective, recognizing someone's performance is a great way to activate serotonin for the leader and for the recipient. A simple gesture like a handwritten note congratulating an employee creates a feel-good factor for both the leader and the team member as serotonin is activated. In fact, it is in the leader's interest to look out for good work and recognize performance.

Oxytocin, the empathy chemical, is activated when people experience friendship, trust and kindness. It is also known as the powerhouse chemical as it can suppress the ill effects of other selfish chemicals. From a leadership perspective, it implies spending quality time with their team members and genuinely investing in their careers without expecting anything in return.

Cortisol, the big one, is often the evil chemical. By design, it is activated during times of crisis or stress to keep the body alert to danger. Its implications are that regular functions start underperforming and excessive cortisol leads to an individual not trusting anyone. More than anything else, cortisol reduces the positive impact of serotonin and oxytocin. From a leadership perspective, leaders who expose their teams to long working hours, stretched targets, aggressive timelines inherently create an environment of mistrust, low productivity and adverse morale.

The managerial interpretation in keeping employees safe can have tremendous business benefits.

The chemical analysis of a leader suggests that the primary role of a leader is to make his employees feel safe (high serotonin, high oxytocin, low cortisol). Such a safety net is not restricted to the C-Suite but to every person in the company as the lowest in the hierarchy often end up facing the customer or the supplier. If the employees feel safe and comfortable, they can ward off danger internally, from competition and the market. In addition, when employees feel safe and comfortable in their working environment, they tend to take risks and don't fear failure. Just think of how many blockbuster products of Google have come from outrageous ideas by employees developed during their 'non-work' time.

Building an environment of high cortisol, implying high stress, can be extremely counterproductive. Think of a cut-throat investment banking or a management consulting firm where employees are trying to outdo each other to move ahead (high cortisol, low serotonin, low oxytocin). Such an environment often leads to high attrition, poor employee morale resulting in poor business performance. Excessive cortisol can also prove detrimental to a person's health. In fact, more and more research in Europe is advocating reducing working hours in service-oriented firms to 40 hours a week. Anything more is counterproductive to business besides promoting mistrust, attrition and poor morale.

In conclusion, biology suggests that keeping employees safe and stress free is the primary job of a good leader. While driving teams to stretched deadlines, building healthy competition and pushing employees outside their comfort zone are modern-day leadership gospel truths, the underlying foundational biology of following such an approach is highly suspect.

Genuinely treat your people well and they will reward you disproportionately. Treat them like Ashish Raman and you will get poisonous buns in return.

35 | SELLING CEMENT LIKE IPHONES

Katrina Kaif, brand ambassador of a cement company, talks about her favourite cement brand in her latest TV ad. Viewers and her fans flock to 'like' the page of the cement company on Instagram. The marketing manager of the cement company actively tracks the brand recall of the cement company and the 'likes' on the Instagram page.[46]

Does this scenario sound ridiculous? Probably Yes.
Is it actually ridiculous? Probably Yes.
Is it farfetched? Probably Yes. But it is not farfetched as far as the implicit transformation that is required.

Focusing solely on cost leadership might not be enough for commodity businesses.

Most commodity businesses, rightly so, have historically focused on staying cost leaders. Cost leadership has been seen as the single biggest criteria for sustainable success. Their core belief of '*I can sell whatever I produce*' has held them in good stead over many decades.

However, many commodity industries have bled in the last few years with multiple market challenges—excessive supply, entry of cheap imports and the global decline in commodity prices. In case of such a complex commodity market, focusing solely on cost leadership will fail to achieve significant dividends. Commodity industries will struggle to rake in the moolah in the upcoming growth cycle if they focus solely on prices and discounts. A mindset shift to move towards an FMCG-like firm with sound focus on sales and marketing over the next few years can help commodity businesses sell more and sell better.

Driving distribution excellence, building channel partner loyalty, premiumization will be critical elements in transforming sales and marketing capabilities.

Driving channel excellence is of paramount importance to build sales and marketing effectiveness. Increasing reach through number of outlets, driving metrics like numeric and weighted distribution should be targeted rigorously. To ensure quality engagement with trade partners, a dedicated trade partner engagement program should be implemented. With an expected uptick in infrastructure and industrial growth, the industrial B2B channel will prove to be a key growth lever. Focus via a dedicated team, product differentiation, superior service, R&D and innovation will be the key to tap a disproportionate share of this growing channel.

The importance of marketing, primarily ATL, is bound to increase in the next few years if commodity companies need to attract more customers. In markets where price is the only differentiator, quality ATL is extremely effective to charge a premium by differentiating on buyer values. In case of cement, many companies have started investing heavily in ATL—JK Cement, Binani Cement (featuring Amitabh Bachchan), Ambuja Cement and so on. In fact, companies with superior brand equity are charging a premium of ₹5–10/ bag from their nearest competitor.[47]

Effective freight management is a no-brainer. In case of most commodity companies, outbound freight constitutes over 25–30 per cent of their cost structure. Well known themes like long-term contracts, fact-based negotiation, optimized total vendor cost, centralized freight management should be looked at. Owning your own fleet of vehicles is also an option that is constantly explored. However, a lot of these are easier said than done as certain fleet operators can prove to be nefarious, especially during the peak agricultural harvesting season.[48]

Process of Change Management Is Always Tricky

For large scale sustainable transformation, process of managing change is extremely critical and can be very tricky. The primary change will be in the mindset of commodity industries having to actively reach out for customers rather than the other way around. The age-old commodity business maxim of *'I can sell whatever I produce'* has to change to *'I can sell only what the customer wants to buy'*.

In conclusion, 'cost leadership' has served many conglomerates (e.g., cement, tyres, apparel, steel) well over the last few decades. However, with increasing market complexity, commodity businesses will need to adapt FMCG like sales and marketing principles to sell more and sell better.

In a decade's time, we might actually see Katrina Kaif advertising for a cement company and thousands flocking to the cement company's Instagram page.

THE ART AND SCIENCE OF CREATING ANALYTICS DASHBOARDS

At a recent interaction at a premier business school, a Business Head proudly proclaimed that he tracked 150 metrics to keep abreast of the nuances of his business. He spoke extensively on how taking decisions solely based on data gave him confidence and a sense of hope.[49]

The 'Give me More Data' syndrome, although ideal, can be counterproductive to taking business decisions, especially when speed of execution and prompt response is necessary or when multiple variables exhibit opposite trends. The chapter looks at the modern-day management information system in a data heavy world.

The age-old adage of 'more data translates to better decisions' can be tricky, at best.

It is common to see the finance department in proprietor-driven firms churning out tens and hundreds of pages of management reports at the beginning of every month to throw unending light on the performance of the previous period. Although exhaustive in nature, the never-ending set of charts and near infinite metrics rarely provide a quality narrative on tracking the 'pulse' of any business. It is only a matter of time before stakeholders lose interest reading such numerically heavy booklets.

In contemporary companies, massive excel sheets with a dozen tabs or complicated software churn out hundreds of reports. With technology, each metric is shown at half a dozen cuts to ensure that the human brain has to potentially track 1,000 numbers before taking any action. In addition, these software even go one step ahead to link these reports to mobile and tablet platforms to help generate business insights 24×7. However, never-ending data analysis can lead to an oft-heard phenomenon aptly titled 'analysis paralysis'.

While data is considered king, and rightly so, more data need not lead to taking better decisions. More data implies more sources resulting in more effort to enter, clean and maintain. In case of qualitative information, it results in the field team spending critical time on data entry rather than customer interactions. More data can sometimes lead to missing out on timely practical execution.

The 'less is more' principle, applied beautifully to user interface design, is apt for designing management information systems too.

Many political leaders, (Reagan, Churchill, etc) and premier FMCG firms like P&G have reiterated the benefit of the one-page memo (also called the 'Decision Cockpit'). Their rationale is that one page should be good enough to communicate the idea or the complexity of the situation. Many business leaders have adopted this philosophy to drive their management information systems. They take a printout of one page, go through it in 60 seconds, and are ready to execute their daily plans.

The *10 KPI rule* is an adaptation of the above approach. The stakeholder identifies 10 most important KPIs for him and tracks those rigorously. Not more. Not less. As a practice, it is advisable that the KPIs are controllable in nature and have a good mix of lead and lag metrics. While it is good to track uncontrollable metrics, their day-to-day utility is questionable.

Like with most things in corporates, even management

information systems should be developed in a role-based fashion. While there is a school of thought that believes that everybody should see similar information for taking business decisions, it is important that users track information which is at their line of sight. For instance, CEOs and members of the board will be most interested in financial, regulatory and market landscape while functional heads will be most interested in operational day-to-day metrics. A well-designed system should ensure that the strategic metrics flow seamlessly into the operational metrics.

Another idea that has increasingly gained traction over the last few years is *Management by Exception*. While the business can track 150 KPIs, the leader tracks only the variables that are outside the pre-defined control limits. It is a practical way to get to the problem area early.

In addition, firms are trying to monetize the deviation of the variable from the defined control limits. While it is difficult, it tries to ensure everybody in the company has a bottom-line perspective.

Finally, it is important to play according to the maturity of the industry the entity is operating in. For instance, if a company is struggling to track its basic sales, developing a strategy to track counter potential for its retailers might be uncalled for. *In simple language, if you are learning how to play at Shivaji Park, avoid trying to ask for a methodology on how to play Wasim Akram on a swinging Old Trafford pitch.*

In conclusion, a well-designed management information system doesn't pride itself on being exhaustive but intuitive, quick and manifests the principle of 'Less is More'. In most business situations, speed of execution and timely practical response to a critical situation is more important than an ideal response. Even today, Winston Churchill's principle of the 'one-page memo' to take decisions works extremely well.

37 | WHEN IN ROME, DO AS THE ROMANS DO

Business travel of management graduates is primarily focused around the western economies along with South East Asia. The work and societal cultures of these places are largely similar and can appear homogeneous to travelling professionals. However, over the last few years, due to increasing trade, travel to other prominent Asian economies has leapfrogged. Some of these nations are vastly different in cultural and societal norms and can be very tricky for first-time professionals. Minor harmless gestures can leave a devastating impact on the fate of business dealings. The chapter looks at some interesting nuances of their culture.[50]

One of the erstwhile great economies in Asia, Japan, is a unique cultural establishment altogether. Their work culture is often characterized by brutally long-work hours with a strong emphasis on loyalty and social order. A friend of mine once described his business trip to Japan. He was sitting with his colleague across the table with his trade partners. The trade partners were a team of 12 people seated neatly conforming to hierarchy with the lady sitting at the extreme end. Nobody spoke out of turn, only the boss did. Nobody dared to speak when their boss was present. Everyone addressed each other as '*San*'. The interesting part in the discussion unfolded when my friend asked the partners to sign a contract on the agreed upon terms. Everybody shuddered at his suggestion with a near explosive situation manifesting itself at the discussion table. As he realized, the word '*contract*' was seen with deep contempt in their business circles. My friend was advised, '*we don't have contracts, we only discuss*'. The terms were never really agreed upon and were closed with another round of discussion once the invoice was raised. Professors of business law will be clearly unemployed in Japanese business schools.

Not far from the land of 'contracts are evil' is another economy very similar. The culture of South Korea is a derivative of Japan as the heads and inheritors of Korean *chaebols* or conglomerates (e.g., Hyundai, Samsung) were educated in Japan and imbibed their business principles. However, in terms of working culture, South Korea is a step ahead of Japan. It has the most punishing work culture with anything less than 14 to 16 hours of work considered as slack. People are always furiously typing at their workstations with someone leaving at 7 PM often getting derisive glances. Being busy is often worn with a badge of honour. There are clear boundaries at work and those outside. Nobody leaves office before the boss does. Senior management has a separate lift and often a separate canteen. However, outside work, managers and their juniors are forced to bond and are even encouraged to 'bitch' about their bosses in front of them. It is seen as a massive stress buster. Next morning though, the boundaries at work re-emerge.

Indonesia, the fourth most populous nation in the world, is considered a poorer cousin to its sister 'tiger' economies in South East Asia. Blessed with abundant natural resources, the country has started witnessing an increasing inflow of foreigners for business transactions. Primarily Islamic and staunchly anti-American, discussions raising a toast to anything American are heavily looked down upon. Handshakes are expected to be double handed with visiting cards being exchanged with both hands and a slouching shoulder as a mark of respect. Loud voice is perceived as 'American' and 'rude', everybody talks in a low voice with discontent shown with extreme diplomacy. Similar to Japan, every person is addressed as '*Pa*'.

In conclusion, every country is unique with respect to its working and societal culture. While most western economies exhibit similar cultural aspects, some prominent Asian economies can be surprisingly different. A bit of preparation and consciousness goes a long way in overcoming awkward moments at the workplace. After all, one man's meat is another man's poison.

38

THE MENTALIST

Professional services (e.g., consulting, finance and banking), in a nutshell, is about building trust-based long-lasting relationship with CXOs (e.g., CEOs, CFOs, COOs). Although problem solving or analytical rigour is often stressed upon as the key skill required to succeed in this industry, successful client interactions go a long way in establishing lucrative professional relationships. Leveraging primitive psychology, as a tool, can be extremely helpful in this exercise.[51]

The most talked about management research on behavioural communication, by researchers Mehrabian, Wiener and Ferris, concluded that 55 per cent of all communication is through body language. Only 7 per cent of all communication is through the actual words spoken while 38 per cent of communication occurs via tone of the voice.

This chapter looks at some of the most extensive techniques leveraging behavioural psychology to garner initial and capture sustained share of mind of CXOs.

Building 'cultural familiarity' and delivering 'impact statements' are often used to garner initial share of mind of CXOs.

Garnering initial share of a CXO's mind is seen as a good starting point in any conversation. Conversation starters to build 'cultural familiarity' with CXOs often revolve around conversing in a local dialect or engaging in a discussion of a sporting tournament or sporting heroes. Other techniques to build 'familiarity' include talking about the stock price of the client or a latest news item featuring the client.

Another technique recommended by management literature includes using an impact statement. The concept of an impact statement revolves around starting a conversation with a key fact or anecdote that can force an audience into thinking about what is coming next. For instance, *'while you are doing well today, nearly 70 per cent of today's customers will no longer be with you in three years' time'* is a classic case of using a 'scare message' as an impact statement.

Utilizing social styles is one of the most effective management tools to capture sustained share of mind of CXOs.

While garnering initial share of mind is easy and achievable, generating a sustained share of mind is significantly more challenging. One of the key management tools that is universally applied by service professionals is the social styles behavioural model. Social styles, formulated by Merrill and Reid, is one of the premier behavioural style models to understand interpersonal behaviour.

Every person's interpersonal style, when evaluated on two key parameters of 'Assertiveness' and 'Emotional Responsiveness' can be categorized in four categories—Expressive, Driver, Analytical and Amiable. People with an Expressive social style tend to look at the 'feeling based' big picture with a slight aversion to excessive detail. People with a Driver social style are result oriented with low emotional display. People with an Analytical social style are process oriented, thorough and fact obsessed. People with an Amiable social style are primarily people focused.

CXOs belonging to a certain social style prefer a particular style of communication. For instance, different strategies can be employed to present a detailed market entry strategy to CXOs. An Analytical social style might be shown a detailed number heavy presentation with the focus on key assumptions and underlying numerical logic. A Driver social style might be shown a detailed implementation plan and the date by which she or he can start realizing profits. An Amiable social style might be presented the people impacted and the softer aspects of business. An Expressive social style might be presented one slide with the key findings. One of the perennial rumours in consulting are about how an Expressive CXO was once a shown the output of a market entry strategy by showing a tree with fruits where each fruit indicated a different segment and the diameter of the fruit indicated the size of the segment. Some of the segments which were immediate priority were shown as low-hanging fruits.

While it is difficult to generalize, there are some behavioural aspects that are characteristic of certain social styles. Expressive and Amiable tend to be emotionally open rather than Analytical and Driver. Expressive and Amiable tend to be great motivators for the people who work for them. Analytical and Driver tend to be more structured, pragmatic and thorough with what they do.

With consistent training, it is possible to assess the social style of a person in less than a minute.

Over a period of time, some management professionals become experts at understanding behavioural psychology.

Basic psychology suggests that non-verbal or behavioural aspects emerge from the 'unconscious' or the temporal lobes of the human brain. These aspects manifest itself in individuals, all individuals behaving in either 'freeze, flight or fight modes'.

With sustained training, experience and exposure, some professionals become experts at behavioural psychology. They become experts at understanding nuances about human behaviour and understanding the root mode behind the 'subconscious communication'. Sample examples include closely following eye movement, noticing the direction of the feet on the floor, twitching of fingers, inclination of posture and so on. Some even try and leverage graphology or critically evaluating the handwriting of the client stakeholder to get a better idea about their state of mind. In fact, a CXO's signature speaks volumes of his mental makeup whether he is stingy, flamboyant, meticulous and so on.

In conclusion, in any client-facing business, building relationships based on trust leads to lasting professional success. Effective interactions based on behavioural psychology can go a long way in succeeding in such a client context. Although it is easy to understand the nuances of some of the management frameworks, building expertise is a matter of specialized coaching and experience.

39

THE FUTURE OF CORPORATE GOVERNANCE

The newspapers, over the last few months of 2019, have been flooded with news of leading corporates engaged in misdemeanours with regard to unfavourable corporate governance. Whether it is about questionable related party transactions or granting loans to entities with conflicts of interest or financial jugglery while reporting annual statements, corporate India is clearly far behind from the requisite level of corporate governance. This takes deafening proportions as the default by one entity (e.g., IL&FS) can lead to an economy entering a full-blown slowdown phase. Interestingly, it is not about education of the executive leading the company as IIM-educated CEOs leading private banks have landed up in a similar soup. This chapter looks at the evolution of corporate governance mechanisms employed till now and the necessary steps required going forward to make the world a little more even of a place.[52]

A simple search on Google suggests that Taylor Swift generates twice the number of hits as the term 'corporate governance'. It tells a lot about our mindset and what we prioritize.

Existing governance vehicles have comprised of board reform, technology to power-up bourses and the stick approach.

There have been various reports on board reform in Indian companies, from the Cadbury report to the recent Uday Kotak report. Suggestions have ranged from mandating a minimum number of independent directors, minimum number of women directors, making all directors fully responsible and splitting the power centres by deploying a separate chairman and CEO. While some of these have been implemented in a fair degree of spirit, some of them are token implementations (e.g., number of women directors). As voices for more robust governance emerge stronger, it is only a matter of time before board reform accelerates to the next gear.

With most aspects in business, technology has always enabled a system of fairer governance. Whether it is the bourses going online after the Harshad Mehta scam or all companies employing billing software for sales and expense control, technology-based solutions have made the world a tiny bit more transparent. However, technology only remains an enabler and is at the risk of manipulation by its human masters.

No developed economy is insulated from the vagaries of misbehaving corporates. The stick approach, or fines, has been heavily deployed in advanced economies. Companies like Facebook, Volkswagen, British Petroleum have had to shell out billions of dollars for mismanagement or lack of adequate control. While the system of fines remains questionable, the 'stick approach' has to make a meaningful debut in India with corporate fines having been restricted to token contributions.

Going forward, in addition to strengthening existing systems, incentives for stronger governance, protecting data and employees will emerge the main driver of governance.

Self-regulation, the world over, is emerging as an important tool to drive requisite corporate behaviour. Whether it is the mutual fund industry or the media conglomerates or e-commerce, the concept is generating the necessary share of eyeballs. An associated corollary is the carrot approach for strong corporate governance. Inspired by the success of the Novo Mercado (new listing segment) on the Bovespa (Brazilian stock exchange), the National Stock Exchange (NSE) is introducing a new category for well-governed firms that voluntarily comply with good corporate governance practices rewarding them with enhanced visibility and liquidity.

With corporate valuations increasingly turning dependent on Black Swan events (one instance of a data leak, one disgruntled employee or one irate politician), managing them will become an increasingly important element of corporate governance.

Over the last few years, there has been an increasingly legalization of lobbying roles at conglomerates the world over. This trend is bound to continue with millions exchanging hands in salaries to ensure a favourable regulatory and political environment. For instance, it always hurts a company when the political head of the state is tweeting against the company every day.

There is no need to introduce the need for data security. From Facebook to Ashley Madison (look up if you don't know what I am referring to), data leaks can cost companies billions in fines and irreparable damage in imagery and equity. Employing a very strong governance mechanism to protect data is going to be hygiene in the days to come and will be personally monitored by corporate boards.

In the age of depressed citizenry looking to make a cause out of everything on social media, it takes one worker, disgruntled or just, to damage a corporate empire (e.g., Uber, various movie studios, Infosys). It will emerge as the single biggest governance prerogative for corporate boards and companies to keep their employees happy, not just lip syncing but genuinely implementing what is necessary.

In conclusion, the system to drive human behaviour to an acceptable level of compliance consists of carrot-oriented rewards, recognition, positive peer pressure and ultimately employing the stick approach. This ecosystem has to function employing all the above-mentioned levers. However, humans being the humans, they can break any system ever designed. Remember *The Shawshank Redemption*?

PERSONAL FINANCE

MANAGING YOUR OWN MONEY

It is a universal truth that nothing makes the world go around like money. However, what is also a universal truth is that most millennials have no or very basic understanding of money market instruments and how to save their limited salaries after their Instagram inspired lifestyles. In all my discussions with them at work or after, understanding and managing your personal finances has always emerged as one of their biggest regrets with the education system in India or at their place of work.

This primer attempts to elaborate on the various money market instruments that are available for personal investment and assist millennials in building a simple charter on where to invest their hard-earned savings.

After all, the more money you have with you, the better you will sleep at night.

Money is better than poverty, if only for financial reasons.
Woody Allen
renowned American comedy writer

If you would like to know the value of money, try to borrow some.
Benjamin Franklin
one of the founding fathers of the United States

40 A FOOL AND HIS MONEY ARE SOON PARTED

In most surveys about millennials, personal finance emerges as the key pain point for them. A key element in this is the limited basic understanding about various financial instruments. A financial instrument or an asset class refers to an investment that has a particular risk or return profile (e.g., fixed deposit [FD], shares). Various asset classes or financial instruments have different risk and return objectives. This chapter looks at the various financial instruments available for investment (refer to Figure 40.1).[53]

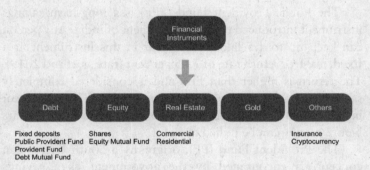

Figure 40.1: An Overview of Various Financial Instruments. Unfortunately, Your Gym Membership Is Not a Financial Instrument

Debt Instruments: Take a Loan from Me and Pay It Back with Interest, without Fail!

A debt instrument originates when person A lends money to person B and in return gets an interest payout for lending that money to B. Person B, who is receiving the loan, can be a corporate, a bank, the government or an individual.

Some of the key debt instruments include FDs, public provident fund (PPF), provident fund (PF) and debt mutual funds.

A fixed deposit (FD) is when you lend your money to a bank and the bank pays you an assured interest rate (typically between 5% and 7%). The bank in turn uses your money to issue loans at a higher interest rate (typically between 8% and 10%) and captures the income on the difference. The difference in what the bank charges for issuing a loan and what it pays you for your FD is termed as net interest margin and is the primary source of earning for any bank. Fixed deposits have the lowest return amongst debt instruments but the highest rate of safety amongst all the debt instruments.

The Public Provident Fund (PPF) is a long-term savings instrument introduced by the Government of India. Any person can keep up to 1.5 lakhs every year in this instrument at a fixed, tax-free return rate of 7.65 per cent (rate as of end 2019). The return is higher than FDs and is considered completely safe as it is backed by the government of India. The investment in PPF needs to be made for a minimum period of 15 years before money can be pulled out of it.

The Provident Fund (PF), originally a South East Asian concept, is encouraged by the government as a savings instrument for building a retirement corpus. The employer and the employee contribute 12 per cent of the employee's basic pay every month to this corpus—do not be elated, both are part of your total pay (or CTC) which the company pays you. The instrument has a highest tax-free return (8.65% as of end 2019) amongst the various debt instruments. The government is unlikely to reduce this rate of return fearing backlash from various labour unions. As an employee, if you find this instrument attractive, you can contribute more every month to it as part of Voluntary Provident Fund (VPF). The fund is largely illiquid before retirement except in case of exceptional circumstances.

A loan can be offered by the government (e.g., government bonds), corporates (e.g., Future Group offering a loan at a certain interest) or a bank (e.g., home loans). A debt mutual fund invests in a combination of government issued loans (also termed as securities or bonds) or corporate-issued bonds. A mutual fund typically invests in 20+ instruments rather than 1 instrument alone to better manage risk and return. For instance, a debt mutual fund can invest in corporate AAA rated bonds (e.g., companies with the highest credit rating), credit risk bonds (e.g., companies that can default on their loans taken but pay a higher interest rates), dynamic bond funds (e.g., mutual fund manager takes a bet on the bond prices basis expected interest rate movements and then allocates money), short-term bonds (e.g., government securities issued for less than three months). Debt mutual funds tend to be more volatile in their returns than fixed, PF or PPF instruments but have a tax benefit after three years.

It is advisable to have at least 50 per cent of total savings in debt instruments at every point in a person's career. Especially as our economy keeps moving around haphazardly. Investing in PPF and PF are no-brainers for any millennial while the choice for FD and debt mutual fund is about individual preference and risk ability.

Equity: You Are a Tiny Owner in a Corporate, Really Tiny!

Equity instruments involve buying a share in a company and being able to take a proportional share of the company's profits. You, as an equity owner, are a small owner of a very large company.

Historically, equities have grown in line with the nominal GDP of a country, equivalent to real GDP + inflation, and hence are considered a very good asset for overcoming inflation. While they have been glamourized for their potential returns, they tend to be extremely volatile and can take a decade to churn out even average returns. It has to be remembered that there is no guaranteed return from equity investments—if the company you have invested in does well, you get rewarded else your investment sinks.

For instance, you can choose to buy a share of a particular company (e.g., Hindustan Unilever Limited). A company can reward you by paying you a dividend from its profits (termed as dividend yield) or the gains you can make from the price increase of that share (termed as capital gains). Shares are traded on the financial market exchanges—two major ones in India being the Bombay Stock Exchange (BSE) and the National Stock Exchange (NSE).

A mutual fund (e.g., HDFC, ICICI, Aditya Birla) is a financial institution that invests your money in a pool of shares for a small charge, typically 0.5 per cent of the fund size. The benefit of mutual funds is that it invests in a lot of various shares and other asset classes like debt. In addition, the fund managers tend to be more professional and have an array of financial tools and research at their disposal. Various types of mutual funds are equity (large cap, mid cap, small cap), debt, hybrid (combination of debt and equity), international markets (e.g., investing in the US equity markets) and so on. For instance, the HDFC Top 100 mutual fund invests in the Top 100 shares by market capitalization listed on the stock exchanges.

For risk avoiders who detest everyday volatility in prices, they shouldn't invest more than 20 per cent of their total savings in equity instruments while risk seekers can choose to put a higher percentage. Although, they should never cross 50 per cent of their total savings in equity instruments.

Gold: When in Doubt and Trouble, Buy without a Blink!

When in doubt, 'buy gold' has been an investment philosophy for most Indian households. India, as a nation, is one of the highest consumers of the yellow metal. Gold is bought as biscuits, as jewellery on key festivals (e.g., Diwali, family weddings) and more recently in terms of gold bonds on the financial markets. Gold is seen as a safe haven, when other financial markets decline (e.g., shares), gold prices tend to rise. In the current set of things, gold has seen a phenomenal rally in prices as there is concern on the condition of the economy and the share prices of various companies. As an asset class, the returns from gold over a 10-year period haven't been great (less than 6%). Although a lot of Indian households stock up a significant proportion of their financial investments in gold, it is advisable not to put more than 5 per cent of total investments in gold.

Real Estate: You Have Not Made It in Life unless You Have Your Own House!

For most Indians, real estate has been the primary source of financial investment. This is due to the psychological safety of holding a property for staying oneself or for the purpose of investment. The return from a real estate investment is a combination of rental yield (annual rents/purchase property of apartment or land) and capital appreciation (increase in price of apartment or land itself).

While residential real estate (e.g., homes where you and I stay) had seen good capital appreciation till a few years back, it has remained stagnant or has declined in the key metros. This is due to the large inventories of unsold apartments of big developers coupled with the reluctance of consumers to buy due to a slowing economy and unreasonably high prices.

In addition, real estate has problems with illiquidity, you won't get a buyer immediately, along with excess supply of apartments in most cities. One of the biggest roadblocks in residential real estate is the concept of low rental yields, for instance a two crore property in Mumbai will get you a monthly rental of about ₹60,000 which translates to an annual rental yield of 3.6 per cent (₹60,000 rent per month × 12 months/2 Crores) and 2.5 per cent (30% tax in the highest slab) after income tax. This yield is significantly lower than other instruments which are at least in excess of 5–6 per cent.

However, commercial real estate (e.g., corporate offices) has been on the rise in India over the last few years. This is being driven by the rising services sector (e.g., IT, BPO) in India along with the incredible number of start-ups that all need quality office space.

For most millennials, real estate should only be considered for the purpose of staying. As an investment vehicle, it is a poor idea due to illiquidity and suboptimal rental yields along with unfavourable tax treatment. In fact, in metros like Mumbai, it is a more sensible option to rent out an apartment rather than buy one and be burdened with a massive loan.

Insurance: Buy a Magic Weapon to Protect from Unforeseen Crisis!

Insurance is a system where the risk of damage is transferred from a person seeking insurance (like you and I) to an insurance company for the payment for a small amount termed as premium (refer to Figure 40.2).

As indicated, the insurance company (e.g., HDFC, ICICI) pays the person requiring insurance the amount in case of an unfortunate event like death or theft in exchange for a small premium. Insurance can be claimed for your property, your

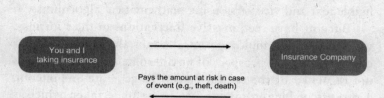

Pays a small premium for
insuring property, life, health

You and I
taking insurance

Insurance Company

Pays the amount at risk in case
of event (e.g., theft, death)

Figure 40.2: The Exchange between You and the Insurance Company. Notice, the
Insurance Company Is Always Placed a Little Higher Than You

medical treatment or for accidental death. If the insurance is
for a certain number of years and the person seeking insurance
meets accidental death within those years, it is called term
insurance, term implying a certain number of years. The
insurance company makes its operations viable as it insures
a large number of people but only a fraction of them end up
claiming the amount at risk. This is mathematically termed as
the law of large numbers.

Everyone should have a medical insurance for themselves
and their family members. Having a life and property
insurance are contingent on levels of safety desired.

Cryptocurrency: Why Need a Poker Table When You Can Gamble Away at Crypto!

Cryptocurrency is a part of a larger ecosystem of alternate financial instruments termed as digital currencies. It is a
decentralized system, operating on the basis of a peer to peer
electronic cash system. Bitcoins are the most famous alternate cryptocurrencies for being in the news for the right and
the wrong reasons. This currency is generated and regulated

using the principles of cryptography. In its most basic form, cryptography translates to converting plain text into unintelligible text and vice versa using mathematical algorithms.

Bitcoins have seen massive fluctuations in their intrinsic value along with multiple central banks showing their clear displeasure at the prospect of an alternate currency which is not regulated by the central banks. To generate one bitcoin, a process of bitcoin mining has to be undertaken which is dependent on sophisticated computer hardware. For instance, it costs nearly 5,000 USD to mine a single bitcoin in the United States. As an individual, it is best advisable to steer clear of these investments before governments and central banks accept this currency the world over.

Others: Weapons of Mass Financial Destruction!

There are other derived asset class termed as financial derivates. A financial derivative is a contract between two parties basis an underlying asset (e.g., bonds, stocks). Some of the primary types of financial derivatives include futures, forwards, options and swaps. Derivatives have been infamously termed as weapons of mass financial destruction by legendary investor Warren Buffett as they can rake in significant gains but can wipe out the entire underlying asset in a matter of seconds. A large part of the 2008 financial crisis failure was attributed to the misuse of financial derivates. Let us leave this section at this. Hopefully you won't have to deal in this.

In conclusion, knowledge of basic financial asset classes is the key before any portfolio decisions can be made for you and I. In the next chapter, we explore how to deploy these various financial instruments to make your money multiply every day. Just like your neighbour's tummy!

Interesting Information about the Financial Markets

How Do the Major Stock Exchanges in India Calculate a Headline Number for Themselves?

The major stock exchanges in India are the Bombay Stock Exchange (BSE) and the National Stock Exchange (NSE). Financial newspapers regularly report headline numbers for stock exchanges (e.g., BSE crosses 40,000). For the BSE, this number is an index of the market capitalization, calculated as the number of shares available to be purchased multiplied by the price of each share, of the Top 30 companies divided by the market capitalization of the Top 30 companies in the year 1978 (taken as 100 to calculate the index):

BSE index value = Market capitalization today (No. of shares available to be purchased × Price of each share for the Top 30 companies) × 100/Market capitalization in a base year of 1978.

Even within the BSE, there are other index numbers reported, BSE mid cap, BSE small cap, BSE banking index and so on. Stock exchanges the world over use the index method to represent their headline numbers.

There Is so Much Written the World Over about the Bond Markets. How Exactly Do They Work?

A bond, or a request for a loan, is typically issued by the government (central or state) or a company (e.g., Mahindra & Mahindra) and the money is provided for by institutions like mutual funds, pension funds, you and I. Once a bond has been issued (termed as primary market), it can be traded actively where investors like you and I can buy it and see its price move up and down on an everyday basis (termed as secondary market). Traded bond prices are extremely susceptible to interest rates decided by the central bank. Bond prices and interest rates are inversely correlated. This is because if interest rates fall, suppliers rush to save their money in bonds as they offer a higher rate driving their prices higher due to higher demand and hence reducing their yields. Yields reduce when bond prices rise because bond prices are calculated as a discounted cash flow of the future coupon rates discounted by the yield to maturity (In case this sentence sounded like Greek to you, you can choose to ignore it).

When a bond or a loan is issued, the ability of the entity borrowing to repay the loan is extremely critical. This is termed as creditworthiness and is deterred by a credit rating agency (e.g., Fitch, Moody's or CRISIL). The bond markets are regulated by the Securities and Exchange Board of India along with the Reserve Bank of India (RBI). Bond markets are considered safer than equity markets, although they can crash when the credit worthiness of the borrower is suspect. The higher the perceived risk of the borrower, the greater the interest rate the borrower has to offer. In the past, people have made tons of money as well as burnt their hands while dealing with high-risk, high-yield bonds (junk grade bonds). These exciting times have often been captured in financial books like *Liar's Poker* and *When Genius Failed*.

41

MULTIPLYING YOUR MONEY EVERY DAY

Mehak Aggarwal, a fresh MBA from IIM, is earning a package of ₹30 lakhs per annum. After paying for her daily expenses and her education loan, she still has over ₹50,000 a month as disposable income. She is not sure what to do with it. Should she buy the latest phone, tablet, shoe or dress? Or should she just save the way her grandmother is forcing her to?[54]

Fresh MBAs from premier institutes are often plush with new-found monetary freedom. From hefty joining bonuses to large disposable incomes, they are often not sure what to do with surplus funds. A lot of them spend it on the latest gadgets or have money lying in their savings bank accounts. As they are in the prime of their youth, saving for retirement or building a financial corpus often sounds an alien concept to them. However, spending and saving money smartly goes a long way in building an ever-increasing financial corpus. This chapter looks at some of these guiding principles. While most people are aware of these principles, a majority of them fail to implement them.

Almost everyone in their 30s and 40s often wish they had managed their finances differently in their 20s.

Most of your grandmother's money management techniques hold true even today.

While consumer spending has been incessantly lauded in print media as a key driver of economic growth, the benefits of saving as much as you can still hold true. The age-old cliché of saving a fixed percentage of income every month makes immense financial sense. Compounding benefits kick in when savings start early. For fresh MBA graduates who are full of disposable income, a blanket rule of saving at least 50 per cent of monthly income, no matter what, is a great starting point.

Although retirement seems four decades away, it is never too late to start planning for it. While most people think they are in the prime of their youth and retirement is many decades away; early planning for retirement can reap huge rewards and financial stability later on. PF and PPF, without any tax burden and assured returns, are excellent instruments to plan for retirement. A PPF guaranteed return of 8.65 per cent a year amounts to 12.5 per cent return on another asset class that is taxable. A lot of MBAs contribute an amount greater than the stipulated 12 per cent to their PF accounts, via VPF to realize greater gains. Allocations in debt instruments (PF, PPF, FDs and debt mutual funds) at every point should be in excess of 50 per cent of savings.

Needless to say, equity markets have historically returned disproportionate returns over a period of time. It is a great idea to invest a percentage of your savings, not exceeding 25 per cent, in equity markets. Over a period of time, equity markets often return in excess of 10 per cent which is greater than most other asset classes.

In some cases, real estate can end up giving disproportionate gains, some MBA graduates pool in initial capital and buy a plot in fast growing tier 2/tier 3 cities.

As with most things in life, it is most important to plan for key financial goals. Typically, education, car, marriage and home in that order. A detailed extrapolation of future cash flows and requirements will automatically point to the minimum amount to be saved every month.

Other aspects to sound financial management involve keeping an emergency fund with two to three months' salary readily accessible. It is always a good idea to track your expenses daily and start cutting down on the flab. Although most employers provide insurance, it is advisable to get a life/ medical insurance.

On a lighter note, some MBA graduates see their marriage as their soundest financial decision. An equal earning spouse is one of the greatest investments that can be made to securing your financial future. If your wife earns more than you, it is even better!

Pitfalls to sensible money management are many, most people end up making these mistakes anyway.

There are a million ways to spend money carelessly. While most people are aware of these pitfalls, most of them tend to fall prey to it.

Spending substantial income piling up too many fancy gadgets is quite useless. While an odd gadget here and there is necessary for entertainment, spending quarter of a lakh on every gadget upgrade might not be necessary. Self-control is the key in such cases although it is easier said than done. Ensuring a monthly investment plan where a planned lump sum is directly debited from your account is always advisable. Idle money lying in the bank account often leads to useless expenditure.

Using credit cards to fund purchase of such assets is even worse. The interest rates charged by credit cards, in excess of 20 per cent per year, are enormous. Defaulting on these even by a day results in interest penalties and a negative impact on CIBIL score leading to complications later on while applying for a loan. Credit cards should be used to manage working capital for a month and not for borrowing money which cannot be paid back in the immediate period.

While not blowing up your disposable income or your yearly bonus is creditable, not doing anything lucrative with it is also not advisable. Keeping money in savings bank accounts at 4 per cent interest per annum is losing money over a period of time. It is natural to use yearly bonuses to pay back any outstanding loans—the earlier you pay, the more money you save.

In conclusion, although money is not the be all and end all of life, it goes a long way in bringing security and material comfort. With simple smart tactics, young professionals can easily accumulate up to ₹1 crore by the time they turn 30. Having such a corpus serves as a fantastic backup in case someone wants to pursue his true calling in his early 30s. Or to take care of a rainy day.

Mehak decides to save 50 per cent of her salary every month as a habit. Of this, she invests about 60 per cent in debt instruments (PF, PPF, FD and debt mutual funds) and 20 per cent in equity instruments (equity mutual funds) with the remaining amount in gold for her marriage. She uses her joining bonus to clear her education loan. In addition, she has kept two months of salary in an emergency corpus for a rainy day. She doesn't understand cryptocurrency and wisely chooses to stay away from it. She has a medical insurance which is company sponsored.

Finally, she postpones the Rado watch for some time. In a few years' time, the interest on her savings will fund her Rado watch.

INDUSTRY PRIMERS

LEARNING THE ROPES ABOUT YOUR LIKELY JOBS

If you are reading this section, and I hope you have reached till this point, in all likelihood, you work at one of these places—a bank, an e-commerce company, an FMCG company or a consulting firm. Irrespective of whether you are a current employee in these sectors or a prospective one, it is difficult to understand, in simple English, how these industries work and the career paths they actually offer.

This section will take you through industry primers, in terms of how the industry operates and the career paths they provide for FMCG, e-commerce, corporate banks and consulting.

66

Sharma ji's son got a job of one crore.
What is your salary?
Your neighbourhood aunty

Without owning something over an extended
period of time, where someone has a chance to
take responsibility for one's recommendations
and accumulate some scar tissue for the
mistakes, one learns a fraction of what one
can. You can say look, I've worked in bananas,
I've worked in peaches, I've worked in grapes.
But you never really taste it.
Steve Jobs
the guy who makes sexy phones,
on management consultants

99

FMCG: AT THE END OF THE DAY, IT IS ALL ABOUT SELLING SOAP

The FMCG industry is the bellwether of the Indian economy. Almost every person in India has been touched by the FMCG industry in India. It is termed as 'fast' as the consumer goods sold (e.g., toothpaste, shampoo, soap) get sold off the shelves and consumed in a short span of time. This chapter looks at an overview of the industry along with key trends and potential career options in the industry.

The Indian FMCG industry is valued at 100 bn $ and has historically grown 1–2 per cent faster than India's GDP.[55]

The FMCG industry is one of the major industries in India valued at over 100 bn $. It has been growing at 8–10 per cent over the last many years and is one of the Top 5 industries in the Indian economy. Historically, the growth has been driven by increasing consumption by rural India, aspirational middle classes consuming more premium products, rise of alternate channels like Modern Trade/e-commerce and innovation in product and packaging by leading FMCG companies.

The industry is characterized by a significant contribution of rural India at about 40 per cent of sales contribution. In terms of trade channels, modern trade despite the hype and hoopla constitutes still 10 per cent of overall business with e-commerce constituting 2–4 per cent of business. The remaining business is catered to by millions of local *kirana* stores.

The FMCG industry in India is divided into three broad categories—food and beverages, personal care and home care. Table 42.1 shows a brief overview of each of the categories.

Category	% Contribution to FMCG	Subcategory	Key Players and Their Brands
Food and beverages	~46%	Tea, coffee, soft drinks, biscuits, ice-cream, dairy products	• ITC (Aashirvaad, Bingo, Sunfeast) • Amul (milk, icecream, cheese) • Parle (Frooti, Maaza, Parle G) • Nestle (Kit Kat, Maggi)
Personal care	~23%	Hair care, skin care, oral care, bath and shower	• Hindustan Unilever (Sunsilk, Dove, Lifebuoy, Fair & Lovely) • Procter & Gamble (Vicks, Olay, Gillette, Pampers) • Colgate (toothpaste, toothbrush, mouthwash) • Godrej (Cinthol, Godrej No. 1)
Home care	~11%	Laundry, dish washing, insecticide	• Hindustan Unilever (Wheel, Surf, Vim) • Procter & Gamble (Ariel, Tide) • Reckitt Benckiser (Mortein, Harpic, Lysol)

Category	% Contribution to FMCG	Subcategory	Key Players and Their Brands
Others (e.g., tobacco)	~20%	Tobacco	• ITC cigarettes

Table 42.1: Various Categories in FMCG, Their Contribution to FMCG as a Category and the Key Players. Any FMCG Person Worth His Salt Can Recite This Table in His Sleep. What Can You Recite When You Are Fast Asleep?

Key operating metrics to success in this industry include growth, distribution and margins.

Each industry has its nuances when it comes down to key metrics that are reported to measure success. As for FMCG, key metrics for success include growth, both value and volume, along with outlet distribution strength and profitability.

Outlet distribution strength is reported as a combination of numeric distribution (% of outlets in the universe billed by the FMCG company) and weighted distribution (% of big outlets in the universe billed by the FMCG company). Some key marketing metrics include brand equity, top of mind recall of brand. Margins or profitability are tracked at the gross, operating and net margin level.

In the midst of our economic slowdown, FMCG majors are focusing on driving innovation in packaging to drive rural sales, leading efficiency through digitization, focusing on Modern Trade for growth and driving micromarket growth.

Over the last few quarters till this book was entering publishing, the entire economy including FMCGs has been witnessing a deep consumption slowdown. To overcome this structural challenge, FMCG majors are employing the following strategies to beat the consumer demand blues.

Given that rural India contributes to ~40 per cent of the FMCG market and ability to purchase is going down there, many FMCGs are launching smaller innovative packs to eat into the share of the local unorganized players (e.g., Sunsilk shampoo, Cadbury chocolate).[56]

A standard theme has been to leverage technology to drive efficiency, from sales team productivity to assist them to sell more at each outlet to organizational level processes to reduce turnaround time. Despite the consumption slowdown, the organized trade or Modern Trade doesn't seem to have been impacted and FMCGs are expected to focus on that to drive double-digit revenue growth.

Over the last few years, leading FMCGs have embarked on a micromarket approach to cater to local tastes and cuisines. For instance, Unilever has divided the India business into 14 'mini-Indias' as each micromarket has a unique taste, language and demand pattern (e.g., coffee preference in India changes every 200 kms). As part of this exercise, they are defining a customized business model for each micromarket to capture greater share from that micromarket.[57]

A career in FMCG is often seen as a launchpad for future leadership roles across industries.

There is merit in the age-old adage that a few years in an FMCG company prepares you for a leadership role in any company across industries. A quick glance through LinkedIn will indicate that leaders across industries (e.g., e-commerce, commodity industries, paints, electronics) often have a background with an FMCG company early on in their career.

In this industry, any fresh graduate is absorbed as part of the management trainee program. The management trainee program, spanning close to a year, gives graduates exposure to various functions—sales, marketing and supply chain on the basis of short quarterly stints. After the successful completion of the program, graduates take on roles either as part of sales (as area sales managers), marketing (as assistant brand managers) or in supply chain (roles in procurement or supply chain) or in human resources (as plant HR or a role in the head office). Graduates can keep growing in their respective functions or can choose to shift functions, for instance from sales to marketing or from sales to trade marketing, after a period of 2 to 3 years. Most graduates strive to make a shift to marketing roles in course of time.

Culturally, a sales role in FMCG is a very high pressure one with lenient dosages of screaming and shouting from superiors. Although equally stressful, a role as part of the marketing team is often seen in better light due to the appearance of a sophisticated culture. Roles in procurement and human resources are fairly streamlined and are more process than target oriented. Nevertheless, any role across functions in an FMCG company gives graduates excellent exposure to running a business and managing a large workforce with subordinates with over 20 years of work experience. Off late, leading FMCG companies are emphasizing on the need for global mobility and actively encouraging graduates to work in an international environment early on in their career.

For business school graduates, average salaries in leading FMCGs hover around a total package of ₹25 lakhs per annum with a fixed salary of around ₹20 lakhs.

Interesting Facts About FMCG

- Did you know that there are over six million FMCG *kirana* outlets in India?[58]
- Did you know that only 23 per cent of the outlets generate 80 per cent of FMCG sales?
- Did you know that Top 10 per cent of villages generate 75 per cent of the opportunity in rural India?

- Did you know that despite being operational for nearly 20 years, organized trade (e.g., large outlets like Big Bazaar) constitutes only 10–12 per cent of FMCG business?[59]

E-COMMERCE: THE ONLINE EVERYTHING STORE

How Does an E-commerce Company Work?

E-commerce or electronic commerce involves buying goods or services through the internet. This model of business has caught up exponentially over the last two decades primarily due to the rise of Amazon. Consumers often flock to this model as they get lured with the benefits of deep discounts, immense choice of seeing the entire portfolio at one go and convenience as everything is delivered to their doorstep. An e-commerce company can choose to operate as a marketplace, where they only provide a platform where sellers and buyers meet, or they can sell their own goods and services online.

What Are the Various Business Models in E-commerce?

There are various business models that come under e-commerce. An e-commerce model can cater to B2C consumers (like you and I, e.g., Amazon) or a B2B model (e.g., Udaan—where retailers or small businesses are brought online through an online medium). Theoretically, models like Google AdWords, Affiliate marketing and online web series consumption (e.g., Netflix) are also included.

Google AdWords involves Google charging the consumer in case their advertised links are reached to by end consumers.

If a person searches for a keyword, your link comes up, he clicks on it and you pay. There are various payout mechanisms, an advertiser can pay only when you click (cost per click mechanism) or when google manages to show that advertised link to a certain number of end consumers (cost per impression mechanism).

Affiliate marketing involves making a percentage of sales as commissions by promoting products or websites when the sales are made through the internet. A classical example is about Instagram influencers who encourage consumers to buy a product and service which they are posting about.

Online web subscriptions (e.g., Netflix, Amazon Prime, Hotstar) involve providing entertainment content online. Their model works either by charging consumers a fixed amount per year (e.g., subscription model by Amazon Prime and Netflix) or by keeping the service free but making money through advertisements (e.g., YouTube).

How Does an E-commerce Company Make Money?

There are various sources of revenue for an e-commerce company:

- It makes money through a commission on every product sold from its website. Typical margins range between 5 per cent and 25 per cent depending on the product being sold.
- It also makes a related source of revenue by charging sellers for listing their products on their website.
- It can charge money for co-branding products by promoting a seller's products on their website (e.g., Apple iPhones were promoted on Amazon during their launch in 2019).

- There are various services an e-commerce player also provides for which they charge, for example, delivery service to end consumers (e.g., remember those painful delivery charges?) and for providing online services like storage and web cloud (e.g., Amazon web services).

- E-commerce companies often produce their own goods and services, called private labels, and charge consumers for these. For instance, Flipkart has its own fashion line of products or Amazon its own reading device, the kindle. The margins on these items are incredibly higher than what they earn by selling branded items.

- Finally, there is a subscription model for loyal group of consumers that an e-commerce company charges. These are in the form of annual or monthly payouts (e.g., Amazon prime, Netflix subscription).

The Indian e-commerce market is booming driven by the young demographic and increasing internet penetration![60]

The Indian e-commerce market is already one of the largest in the world and is expected to be one of the world's top three markets in the next five years. In terms of growth, the e-commerce market has been growing at 35–40 per cent over the last few years and is expected to growth at over 20 per cent over the next five years. As a percentage of offline retail, the contribution of e-commerce remains low at 1–3 per cent currently and is expected to rise to 5–7 per cent over the next five years.

Although the category started off by selling books (remember the original Amazon?), the big categories selling on e-commerce include electronics (nearly 45% of total turnover) and apparel (nearly 30% of total turnover). The growth of this channel has been fuelled by deep discounts (e.g., Big

Billion by Flipkart) along with a younger technology savvy population and deep penetration of the internet (~700 million active users).

Key e-commerce trends include consumers moving online to offline, a reducing pace of growth as deep discounting reduces and the next 200 million consumers coming from the heartland of India![61]

Although the e-commerce sector is bound to grow leaps and bounds, its rate of growth is expected to stagnate around 20 per cent. As a percentage of overall retail, e-commerce is likely to reach 5–7 per cent from 1–3 per cent currently over the next few years. The major source of growth is likely to be from the real India, from Tier 1 and Tier 2 towns. A major trend that is also emerging is a lot of consumers in metro cities moving to offline (brick and mortar) stores as they prefer the real life feel of what they buy and the lure of deep discounting in e-commerce reduces. This is visible as major online brands like Xiaomi, OnePlus, Flipkart private labels, Lenskart open offline stores.[62]

What Does All This Mean in Terms of a Career Path?

For an aspiring business graduate, careers in e-commerce are along the lines of category management, product development and customer experience. As part of category management (e.g., mobiles), they are responsible for end-to-end operations, from procurement to sales and marketing for that category. As part of product development, they typically work with global teams to roll out an innovative product (e.g., in-house logistics arm for an e-commerce company, payments arm). The customer experience team is like an in-house consulting arm that works on internal projects to drive customer experience. Entry level salaries for business postgraduates are in the range of 25 to 30 lakhs per annum with handsome stock allocation at leading e-commerce companies.

While work cultures at most e-commerce firms are entrepreneurial, involving long hours and intense business pressures, they can be rewarding monetarily and from a learning perspective!

BANKING: MODERN-DAY SHYLOCK, LEND AND EARN

A bank is how it seems in our movies—it has numerous branches, it has ATMs to withdraw cash from, it is painful to visit their branches and get work done and hence people prefer mobile banking. Their agents stalk you over phone, email and WhatsApp like a jilted lover asking you to take a loan, buy an insurance or worst case just a credit card.

The banking industry is the cornerstone of the Indian economy.

The banking industry, in addition to the larger financial services industry, is the cornerstone of any global economy. The chaos and the bloodbath that followed after Lehmann brothers went bankrupt in the 2008 financial crisis is ample indicator of this phenomenon. The Indian banking industry compromises of public (e.g., State Bank of India) and private sector banks (e.g., Deutsche Bank) in addition to local co-operatives. Over the last few years, there has been a proliferation in the rise of payments banks (e.g., Airtel, Jio). They are primarily for storing cash rather than rolling out key financial transactions like lending and credit cards. The framework of banking in India is under the ambit of the apolitical Reserve Bank of India (RBI).

As you would expect, the banks do know how to take, sorry make money after all.

It is interesting to understand how a bank makes money. They make money by loaning out deposits (e.g., your FDs) which you have with them. Money is lent to corporates, large and small, and to individual consumers like you and I. Individual consumers can take a loan to buy a house, a fancy car, sponsor an education or to buy your spouse her dream jewellery!

The rate at which they lend money (termed as MCLR [marginal cost of lending rate]) is higher than the rate they pay you to make a deposit with them. The difference in the rates of lending a loan to an end consumer and paying an end consumer on their deposits with them is termed as net interest margin and is the primary source of income to banks.

In addition, banks also try to leverage their large consumer base and drive other sources of revenue by selling insurance, mutual funds and other products to their consumers. For their consumers who are affluent, termed as high net worth (financial assets greater than $1 million) in banking parlance, private wealth management services are provided. This add-on income which banks try to drive is the reason so many agents keep nagging you day and night.

Related financial entities of banks assist in taking companies public on the stock market and play a platform role in arranging for corporate buyers and sellers to meet and deal with each other. Such exotic entities, charging exorbitant fees, are termed under the garb of investment banking.

Key Operating Metrics Every Banker Worth His Salt Tracks

In addition to basic revenue growth and profitability measures, the following are key metrics that are tracked for healthy operations in a bank:

- **Net interest margin:** As explained earlier, the difference in the rate at which money is loaned out and the rate the bank pays you for your deposit with them.

- **Loan growth:** An increase in growth in money loaned out means greater interest income the bank makes and hence is tracked closely.
- **Non-performing assets:** The metric being gossiped over at all banking page 3 parties. It implies the amount of loans that might be defaulted over by end consumers, and hence will be written off by the bank.
- **Cross sale:** The metric that implies additional services like mutual funds, insurance that are sold to the existing set of banking consumers.

Banks are making an attempt to become the amazon of financial services.

Over the last few years, banks have been at the forefront of driving superior customer experience. Numerous exercises such as internet banking, phone banking, branchless banking, video banking, Aadhar-enabled branch opening, one-click purchase of insurance and mutual funds have gone a long way in consumers having to avoid the hassle of visiting physical branches!

However, banks have often been vilified for their seemingly brash behaviour. Especially in investment banks, the shameless display of wealth along with ludicrous bonuses given as part of banking jobs has often attracted the ire of the mainstream population and the government. The Occupy Wall Street movement[63] in 2011 is a classical example of the anger the general populace felt towards the banking system over their rampant corruption, greed and undue influence over the government. The 2008 financial crisis has often been seen as a result of irresponsible behaviour on part of the banks where they deliberately undertook dubious decisions to make a quick buck rather than worry over the larger good of their consumers!

For a business graduate, a career in banking is full of glamour, glitz, money and can be rewarding at times.

Often business graduates join large public and private banks after their education. Akin to FMCG, they are treated like management trainees for the first 9–15 months where they spend a few months in each desk (e.g., understanding if a consumer is creditworthy for a loan to be given, wealth management for a high net worth individual, selling of credit cards, working with a corporate as a relationship manager). After their rotation is completed, they are absorbed in a particular desk where they keep growing. Entry level salaries for a business postgraduate in private commercial banks is 23–27 lakhs per annum while it ranges around 13–17 lakhs per annum for public commercial banks.

The seemingly fancier roles also include trading and investment banking. As part of the trading arm, freshly educated graduates buy and sell stocks and bonds through the day and pose as glorified agents. As part of the investment banking arms, they assist in companies going public and play a platform role in facilitating corporates looking to buy and sell to each other. Entry-level salaries in trading and investment banking are extremely lucrative and can start from a minimum of 30 lakhs per annum.

Over the last few years, technology-enabled roles at financial technology start-ups are turning in vogue. Product manager roles in firms like Paytm or customer acquisition manager, glorified name for sales, are generating a lot of traction.

Although roles in the banking industry are monetarily rewarding, they come with undue stress, lack of work life balance, immense office politics (think of movies *The Wolf of Wall Street* or *Barbarians at the Gate*), poor sense of ethics (think of how many banking chiefs in India are getting fired) and a deep sense of not doing meaningful work among its employees.

Interesting Facts about the Indian Banking System

- Did you know that nearly 300 million Jan-Dhan Accounts have been opened over the last few years?[64]
- Did you know that Hong Kong and Shanghai Banking Corporation (HSBC) was the first bank to introduce the ATM concept in India in 1987?
- Did you know that there are many banks globally that operate without a physical branch?
- Did you know that retail credit loaned out to Indian banking consumers is in addition of $ 1 trillion?[65] (India's GDP is $ ~2.7 trillion.)
- Did you know that India has one of the largest ATM networks in the world?

MANAGEMENT CONSULTING: GLITZ, GLAMOUR AND DRAMA

With most management consultants, a lot of operations are up in the air with little secondary research backing it. Hence you don't find research links mentioned for most of the points mentioned below.

For readers who do not have a humour bone, I am joking! After all, this industry has fed me for more than a decade.

What Does a Consulting Firm Exactly Do?

This section needs no introduction if you have followed the series *House of Lies*. The series depicts the intricate details of life in a consulting firm. In pedestrian language, a consulting firm is a doctor to any corporate's persisting problem. Problems can be oriented around spiralling costs, tapering growth, stretched aspirations, technological backwardness or anything which they are not capable of doing on their own.

A consulting team of extremely smart graduates, as they would like to believe internally, land up in their fancy suits and prescribe a medication for their sick clients. Consulting projects can either be extremely short (6–8 weeks) or span across years (18–24 months).

Some of the key players in this industry are McKinsey & Company, Boston Consulting Group, Bain & Company, Kearney, Deloitte, PricewaterhouseCoopers, Ernst & Young, Infosys, Tata Consultancy Services, IBM and other players.

Metrics that are tracked in a consulting firm are akin to other service companies.

From a company point of view, the regular elements of financial statements are tracked comprehensively. Key metrics include revenue, number of new and repeat clients, key cost heads like salaries of employees and overall profitability.

From an employee point of view, key metrics include utilization, defined as percentage of time spent on work that is paid for by the client. For senior professionals, at principal and partner levels, sales defined as business that is generated for the company is the primary responsibility.

From a project point of view, key metrics include project revenue, project profit and collections (defined as money that is actually paid).

For a management graduate, the career paths in a consulting firm are clearly defined.

The career path for fresh management graduates includes joining the consulting firm is at an analyst level (or equivalent nomenclature). At this level, they are primarily involved with handling data and excel spreadsheets with limited exposure to the client.

After a period of 2–3 years, they move on to a senior consultant level (or equivalent nomenclature) where they own independent modules in the project and have substantial client exposure.

After another 2–3 years, they move to a project manager level where they own the entire project and manage senior client stakeholders.

After a period of another 3–4 years, the next exotic level they move onto is a principal level where they manage multiple projects and bring in new business.

Extremely successful principals go to become partners after a period of 4–6 years where they head offerings, own a portion of the company and are responsible for driving overall business. Historically, it is believed that once you become a partner, the world blesses you with abundance in money, fame, good looks, cows and buffalos.

It takes anywhere between 8 and 12 years for a fresh management graduate to become a partner in a consulting firm. As you can guess, the real deal is when you make partner!

The Stereotype about Living Out of a Suitcase Is Absolutely True!

The biggest advantage of working in a consulting firm is the nature of exposure driven be the variety of clients and diversity of work that is undertaken by everyone. In a consulting firm, there is never a dull moment as you meet different people, internally and externally, on a daily basis. In terms of career growth, the profession leads to excellent exit options. The compensation is marginally above other lucrative opportunities in FMCG with entry-level salaries for business school postgraduates hovering around 30 lakhs. It might be lower than the astronomical salaries offered by start-up companies. Needless to say, remuneration is lower than what is offered by investment banks.

Despite the exposure and the lifestyle benefits, there are steep downsides to the profession. It is a no-brainer that work hours are brutal. Anyone working less than 70–80 hours a week is a resident of planet Mars. If you abhor travel, you are in the wrong profession. The health implications of living such an unhealthy high-profile life coupled with miserable personal lives (divorce rates amongst consultants are the highest) often lead to a significant portion of the workforce leaving this industry after two to three years.

From an ivory tower approach, the industry is heading towards getting your hands dirtier!

The industry has been notorious for working out of ivory towers and doling out documents as final outputs which clients rarely understood. Over the last two decades, consulting companies have been increasingly walking the talk by implementing their suggestions and agreeing to a profit-sharing deal with their clients (*they make money when their recommendations deliver financial benefit. Isn't that sweet?*). Over the last few years, with an increasing role of technology, analytics and artificial intelligence, they are playing a role of enabling these buzzwords to deliver business outcomes.

Going forward, they are expected to go the venture capital route where they will invest their own money in particular clients, turn them around and rake in disproportionate benefits.

46

BIG BROTHER: HOW DOES THE INDIAN GOVERNMENT WORK?

While everyone is aware and has a point of view on how the government of India works, in reality, it operates as a corporate that reports a P&L statement. It has sources of revenue and spends the revenue it earns in a systematic way. This chapter illustrates how these numbers add up and what the government actively does to control the Indian economy.

The main source of revenue for the government is from taxes, from corporates, individuals and from GST.

There are three main sources of revenue for the government of India—from taxes, non-taxes and other sources. Revenue from taxes constitute nearly 80 per cent of the total revenue while revenue from non-taxes constitute about 15 per cent of the total revenue while the remaining is raised from other sources (refer to Table 46.1).

Revenue from taxes comprises tax levied on individuals like you and I, tax levied on corporates, tax incurred due to GST and tax earned from duties and customs. Customs duties are applied on goods imported and exported while duties are applicable on items not under the purview of GST, namely petroleum and liquor.[66]

Revenue Source	Revenue Head	Description	Indicative % of Total Revenue
Tax	Income tax on individual	Income tax on individual earning	16
	Tax on corporate profits	Tax on corporate profits	21
	Goods and service tax	Read the newspapers, no explanation needed	19
	Duties and Customs	Customs are on items imported and exported while duties are on items not included in GST (e.g. petroleum, liquor)	12
	Others		10
Non-tax	Telecom spectrum revenue	Auction of telecom spectrum network like 3G, 4G, 5G	15
	Dividends from holdings in PSUs	% of profit of public sector units ploughed back to the government	
	Surplus from Reserve Bank of India	Extra amount transferred from the Reserve Bank of India to the government every year	

Revenue Source	Revenue Head	Description	Indicative % of Total Revenue
	Interest on loans to state governments and public sector enterprises		
Other sources	Disinvestment from holdings in public sector enterprises	Amount from government selling its stake in public sector units (e.g. Steel Authority of India Limited, Bharat Heavy Electricals Limited)	5

Table 46.1: Revenue Source of the Government from Tax, Non-tax and Other Sources. Were You Under the Illusion That Running the Country Was an Easy Job?

Source: Ministry of Finance, Government of India.

The revenue earned by the government of India is spent by allocating a portion to states for their operations, running public welfare schemes, operating establishments like defence and necessary subsidies.

Like a P&L statement, the revenue earned by the government is spent by the government to run their daily operations. Key heads of expenditures are indicated below (refer to Table 46.2). The key heads are the public welfare schemes that are run by the government. Some of the more famous schemes are Jan-Dhan, National Rural Employment Guarantee Act, Make in India, Digital India, Ujjwala and so on.[67]

Expenditure Head	Description	Indicative % of Total Cost
Share to state governments	Share of funds allocated to state governments to run their daily operations	23
Interest payment for loans	Interest paid by the government for their borrowings	18
Central government schemes sponsored by the government	Schemes that are run by the government (e.g. digital India, Jan Dhan, Make in India, National rural employment guarantee act	23
Schemes sponsored by the central and the state government		
Defense expenditure	Necessary expenditure to run the army, navy and the air forces	9
Subsidies	Subsidies to support the poor as part of various government programs	8
Pension	Pensions given to retired workforce sponsored by the government	5

Table 46.2: Costs Borne by the Government of India. Do Any of These Items Come as a Surprise to You?

Source: Ministry of Finance, Government of India.

Oh Deficit, My Deficit!

As with most companies, while revenue should be higher than costs incurred, it may or may not turn out to be the case in reality. A situation in which costs are greater than revenue is termed as revenue deficit. Similarly, if the capital disbursements, in the form of large multi-year expenditures, of the government exceed capital receipts, it is termed as capital deficit. Fiscal deficit is the total of revenue and capital deficit and is a key metric that is tracked for measuring financial health of the government. It is often expressed as a percentage of the GDP. In India, the government is targeting a fiscal deficit at 3.3 per cent of its GDP.

To maintain the economic health of the country, the government and the Central Bank (RBI) have a combination of tools at their disposal!

In order to bridge the gap between revenue and expenditure, a prudent government can either raise taxes (increase the percentage of income tax or increase the number of people paying income tax) or monitor its expenses (lower subsidies, defer expenditures or bring in technology to reduce inefficiency in spends).

Meanwhile, the central bank's (RBI) objective is to maintain the targeted inflation (rate at which the prices of goods change every year). The primary method for controlling inflation adopted by the central bank is to influence the money supply available in the system. If it can reduce the money supply, less money chases more goods and hence prices (and hence inflation) decrease. If it increases the money supply, more money chases less goods and hence prices (and hence inflation) increase.

To adjust the money supply in the system, the central bank has three tools at its disposal, setting the repo rate, the cash reserve ratio and the rate of interest it pays to private banks. The repo rate is the rate at which banks can borrow money from the RBI. If the rate is increasing, then banks borrow lesser, loaning out lesser to consumers and hence reducing the money supply in the system (and hence decreasing inflation).

The Cash Reserve Ratio implies the minimum amount a bank should keep its deposits in liquid form (cash). If the RBI wants to reduce money supply in the system to decrease inflation, it can choose to increase the cash reserve ratio for private banks. It can also choose to alter the interest rates it pays out to banks for borrowing their money. To increase inflation, it will decrease the reverse repo rate (the interest it will pay out), and hence making it more lucrative for the private bank to loan out the money and increasing money supply thereby increasing inflation.

YOUR CAREER

GETTING YOUR DREAM EDUCATION AND JOB

For millennials, most things in life revolve around getting admitted into your dream educational institute and securing your dream job. In fact, society judges an individual's success if the three magical letters, IIM or IIT, get attached to somebody's name. Once you get admitted at your desired place of education, your neighbourhood aunty will ensure that you never lose focus on the highest paying job in India. This section will help you satisfy the inner cravings of your neighbourhood aunty.

*Every day I get up and look through the
Forbes list of the richest people in America.
If I'm not there, I go to work.*
Robert Orben
American comedian and magician

*Getting paid to sleep or eating chocolate
would be a dream job.*
Unknown

47

GETTING THE MAXIMUM OUT OF YOUR BUSINESS SCHOOL

Kanika Malhotra, a graduate from Delhi University, is considering an MBA from a US business school. While she is convinced that the MBA program is one of the best investments she can make to accelerate her career, she is perturbed by the question on how she can maximize her ROI from the program. Although she is sure the program will help her, she is not sure how to prioritize her applications among business schools.[68]

One of the most persistent traits of contemporary graduates is the relentless focus on the 'What's In It For Me' (WIIFM) syndrome. From jobs to vacations to relationships to food, the WIIFM syndrome has permeated every aspect of their life.

For MBA aspirants, the question of WIIFM from their MBA program, as measured by the absolute Return or the ROI, is of supreme relevance and importance. The difficulty, however, arises in the definition, the measurement and the guiding principle on what a good return on investment is.

The following chapter tries to look at the various interpretations, seven in total, of the ROI from an MBA program that can be of relevance to an MBA graduate.

It Is All about the Money

In its most primitive form, the ROI is a pure financial measure. The salary earned by the MBA graduate compared to the cost incurred as part of the program.

The Economist recently carried an article about MBA programs with the best ROI. The article looked at the salary given up by the incoming graduate, the cost of the program incurred and the average salary offered to the outgoing graduate.

The article reported that French powerhouse HEC Paris topped the list, with a 66.5 per cent ROI. Here, students gave up $49,788 in salary to participate in the program's 16-month curriculum. Along with its reasonable $61,709 price tag, students graduated into positions paying $123,694, more than doubling their previous salary. The famed Ivy Leagues featured much lower on this list.

Back home, the MBA program offered by the Faculty of Management Sciences has the best ROI. The fees for the entire program is still less than ₹50,000. Contrast this with the fees for the Indian School of Business which charges in excess of ₹30 lakhs. Both have a similar placement record.

To further maximize monetary ROI, graduates can look at opting for MBA programs that are of a shorter duration (e.g., INSEAD France, London School of Business, etc), or enrol for a part-time MBA program.

Knowledge Is Power

Skills in any job are the key. The keystone for success, especially in the first few years of a corporate career, is pure knowledge. Both specialist skills and generalist skills add to one's success.

If a graduate's return is purely defined on this metric, it is not only important to study and get very good grades, but it is also important to look at the larger picture. Developing thought leadership like case studies and publications outside the course curriculum is a great way to build credentials and skills. Working outside the stipulated curriculum will also help establish a great way to connect with the faculty which can reap rich rewards throughout an MBA graduate's career.

The Globally Aware MBA

Travel always helps. Working in different cultures and taking on cross border assignments are essential in developing an MBA graduate's career—especially for taking up senior leadership roles.

There are numerous opportunities a business school offers to take up an international stint and work on a cross-border assignment.

If a graduate's return is defined by the cross-cultural connect developed or the international exposure attained over the period of two years, specific steps are necessary. Examples include enrolling for the student exchange program, applying for summer internships that offer international locations and enrolling for courses which have been developed in association with foreign universities and involve travelling to the foreign university. For instance, IIM Bangalore offers a course that involves studying at Stanford for a period of two weeks.

Exponential Impact

It is fairly obvious the benefits of networking in a graduate's career. Networking with the senior batch, the junior batch, the academic faculty, the alumni can all have benefits. Networking always has exponential benefits in the long run.

If a graduate's return is defined by the number of quality connections developed over the MBA program, it is imperative to choose an institute with a large batch size and where the alumni is strong. Opting for a more recently established school is not the greatest idea.

To build connections, attending social events and alumni interaction events are necessary. It can be of great help to be a part of the student alumni committee. This committee interacts with alumni on a regular basis.

Barbarians at the Gate

The higher echelons of corporate jobs are often dominated by alpha males, barbarians trying to protect their own territory and invade someone else's. To climb the top of the corporate ladder, supreme political acumen is essential. Anything less than supreme political acumen does not suffice. Being competent is just not good enough.

A business school, with its student politics, numerous student activities and tiffs with the administration is a suitable ground for building political acumen.

If your return is defined as emerging politically competent after the MBA program, it makes sense to pick business schools where the process of student elections and student bodies is prominent and given a lot of importance. An MBA graduate should focus on taking part in a wide gamut of student activities.

Spouse Fest

A recent article in a leading newspaper spoke about how graduates are increasingly looking at business schools as a place for spouse hunting. The article even encouraged graduates, especially women, to look for their better halves in business school. The article argued that a business school is one of those rare places where a graduate meets many like-minded people over a period of two years with no parental pressure, no societal pressure and a long time of two years.

If your return is defined as meeting a potential spouse, it makes sense to pick an institute where the gender ratio is above average. The graduate needs to invest substantial time during the two-year program to ensure that his/her aspirational return materializes.

Let's Get a Life

In a lot of business schools, especially in Europe, an MBA is seen as an intermediate two-year holiday before going back to the gruelling corporate world. For stressed, overworked youngsters, the MBA program with its late-night parties, dorm parties, pool parties, international trips, sporting events, social events and so on is seen by many as the perfect two-year holiday.

If an MBA graduate's definition of ROI is measured by the amount of fun he or she has, the right kind of institute should be chosen, where the amount of academic rigour is not very high and where the environment is not a dog-eat-dog world.

In conclusion, most of the ROI metrics are important and significant in their own place. At different stages of an MBA graduate's life, different metrics become the most important. During the MBA program, being fixated on one single ROI metric is not advisable. For an MBA aspirant, it is important to have an above average ROI across most definitions.

It's not all about the money for Kanika. She decides to focus on friends, fun and joining an institute that helps her gaining international exposure. She, accordingly, chooses her institute.

48 GETTING YOUR DREAM JOB IN A BUSINESS SCHOOL

I keep visiting IIM Bangalore across years to address the incoming batch of students on what to expect over the next two years and how to a make the most out of the two-year flagship MBA program. I speak to them about the tremendous equity of the IIM tag, the quality of the alumni, the beautiful campus and Bangalore's unmatchable weather. While they patiently hear me as most incoming students are not impolite to alumni, I always get a sense that I am not addressing what they want to know. In one of the years, one brave incoming student put up his hand, *'can you please let us know how I can get my dream Day Zero job?'* A quick glance around the room indicated that everybody is interested in that question, only that.[69]

You can't blame them. A decade ago in their shoes, I was looking at the answers to the same question. But their situation is worse. The batch size has crossed 450. The economy is recovering at best. There is incredible peer pressure. The fees for the program has been increased to ₹25 lakhs. There is immense probing from the *taujis* (uncles), *mausijis* (aunties) and neighbourhood aunties on when the ₹1 crore package will be sealed. Their matrimonial prospects are linked to their job offer. All of them have been super achievers; there is no question of failure. It is not an option.

Not to anyone's surprise, most business schools are treated like placement agencies. Intangible benefits like knowledge, rich alumni network, brand equity and quality of peers are often long term in nature and ignored by all in the short run. I thought of dodging the question but gave them what they wanted to know.

The following are some of the key principles I spoke of at that session.

To get your dream job, you will need to have a sound resume. A sound resume is not built overnight. It takes smart, consistent effort over two years.

The key question is what is a good resume? Although a common perception is that MBA graduates with extraordinary academic grades have great resumes, I believe that a good resume is a balanced one that has achievements across various dimensions—academics, articles published, sports, positions of responsibility, social impact and so on. To be successful in corporate India and make the most of your two-year MBA, it is important to invest your efforts across as many dimensions as possible.

Different recruiters value different skills on a resume. An investment bank might focus on grades in finance electives and grades in mathematics-based subjects. A consulting firm might focus on academic grades and positions of responsibility. An FMCG firm might focus on industry projects and work done in consumer marketing. It is important for an MBA graduate to have customized resumes for different recruiters.

The emphasis of quality networking in landing your dream job can never be emphasized enough. Networking has exponential short-term and long-term benefits.

A sound resume can take you only a certain distance. After that, it is a matter of quality networking and performance in the interview. Although a recruiter might be impressed with a solid resume, they are always interested in the qualitative feedback about a potential hire. Feedback about an MBA candidate is often sought from the candidate's senior batch, from the professors who have taught them and from the campus team that interacted with the MBA candidate during the placement presentations. After all, familiarity breeds confidence!

For an MBA candidate, it is imperative to develop relationships with seniors who work in the industry of their choice. It is also important to actively engage with recruiting teams that come on campus and reach out to relevant alumni from their desired sectors. Time invested in such activities has a very high return on investment.

A sound resume and quality networking can get you to the doorstep of the interview. A great interview is what will seal the deal.

Irrespective of everything, the final interview is the key to landing your dream job. Nothing gives you a greater chance of performing well at your final interview other than being well prepared for it. Every recruiter expects MBA candidates to be well read on their firm; basic techniques like setting up google alerts on that firm, talking to seniors working in that firm or researching online can go a long way. Recruiters will expect candidates to know their entire resume at the back of their hand. Candidates should be able to speak and defend every point on their resume with logic, passion and enthusiasm.

Specific customized preparation is required for certain type of profiles. Consulting firms expect candidates to be well prepared about case interviews. It makes sense to study the background of the interview panel and be well prepared on those industries they have worked on. A quick LinkedIn check of such panellists is useful at providing such information. Investment banking recruiters will expect MBA graduates to have a sound knowledge of financial derivatives, corporate finance, banking institutions and so on.

Spikes or differentiation is overhyped. In fact, you need to be consistently above average across most dimensions. It is better to be a competent jack of all trades rather than the master of only aspect.

One guiding principle you will always hear during your MBA program and right throughout your career is the need to differentiate. You need to be ahead of everyone else on the bell curve and have one spike that is unmatchable.

In my opinion, the need for differentiation and having a brilliant spike is overhyped. What is important for an MBA graduate is to be a competent jack of all trades. There is no need to be the undisputed number one at everything. It is important to be above average across most dimensions—academics, thought leadership, extracurricular activities, positions of responsibility and so on.

Even if you manage to land yourself your dream job, it is important to have the skills to perform on that job. A business school education gives multiple channels to learn the right set of skills.

To perform consistently in your dream job, it is necessary to build certain skills in business school itself. Blindly enrolling for electives that lead to a high academic grade can be suicidal later on. It is necessary to have a well-rounded set of courses. In my opinion, the following electives should always be taken irrespective of the degree of difficulty involved—spreadsheet modelling, corporate finance, market research, business law, advanced corporate strategy.

It is rudimentary to state that MBA graduates are expected to have good presentation and excel skills. I have noticed there are some MBA graduates who try to avoid giving presentations or avoid making complex excel sheets. Corporates who hire from top business schools expect MBA graduates to be proficient at presenting, making fabulous slides and building complex excel models.

Before all of this, the key to landing a good job is to often ask in which area your interest lies. Building your resume in your area of interest is far easier. The answers to such a question can take a long time.

Towards the end of the session I was asked, 'How do I do what I am good at?' It was one of those questions that warrants a standard answer of following your heart, passion and letting life showing you the way.

However, there is no easy answer to this question. Many people wait for months, years and in some case decades to identify what they are good at and what they want to do. There are certain avenues in business school, however, which can hint at what you might be good at. A summer internship is a great avenue to find out if you like that industry or not. The summer internship, an eight-week live industry program, can give fresh MBA graduates a point of view on the industry and their fit in that industry. If you are not happy with your internship, it is a great avenue to answer what industry you might definitely not like.

Having multiple conversations with your seniors, alumni and professors is a great way to identify your potential area of interest. They can give you their perspectives on various sectors. Attending the presentations of various companies can give you a very good idea.

Once I finished the session, I thought I left them more stressed than when the session started. However, I am sure that they would see the big picture in a few years—the equity of the brand, the richness of the alumni, the quality of the faculty and the positive memories during the two-year journey.

In conclusion, the final placement is only the starting point in a three-decade career and has limited utility. About

40 per cent of MBA graduates make a shift out of their dream jobs within the first three years itself. While it is difficult to isolate yourself from the one-crore *tamasha*, it should always be seen in perspective and not as an existential parameter.

A critical element to landing your dream job is to construct an incredibly powerful resume. The next chapter delves into some of these principles.

Is That So?

1. Did you know that IIM Bangalore stopped reporting salary packages after some students started getting unnecessary harassment calls?
2. Did you know that during the recent recession a number of experienced MBAs accepted jobs that paid less than what they left when they joined the MBA program?
3. Did you know that an increasing number of MBA students are rejecting hefty pay packages and opting for social or entrepreneurial roles?

49

WRITING A DREAM RESUME

Most people find it hard to believe that potential recruiters screen candidates by glancing at their resumes for not more than 45 seconds. Yes, it is in seconds and not minutes.

In a massively competitive environment with limited attention spans while evaluating resumes, it becomes extremely important to develop a good resume that is simple, stands out and communicates key differentiating achievements effectively.[70]

In a nutshell, making your resume involves deliberations along key dimensions like identifying the right structure, building on the right format, using impactful content and preparing for what is outside the resume. This chapter explores some of these themes.

Identifying the Right Structure Is the Most Essential Step while Drafting a Resume

Following points should be carefully deliberated before moving on to the other elements.

- A good resume is always restricted to one page. In case you believe you have done so many things in life that it cannot be compressed in a single page, you should carefully consider that the resumes of Steve Jobs, Roger Federer and Barrack Obama are drafted in a single page.
- The various sections should be arranged in descending order of strength.

- A resume should not have more than three to four sections. For an aspiring management professional, these sections can be academics, work experience, academic and industry projects, extracurricular activities and so on. In case of more senior professionals, it is also advisable to add an 'Executive Summary' section at the top that talks of the four to five key points in the resume which might be of interest to the recruiter.

Using the Right Format Is Critical while Drafting the Resume

Although some of these points are considered basic, missing out on these can render a resume unreadable. Following are some key points that should be considered while defining the format for making a resume.

- A good starting point is to pick a standard template for making a resume. Most word processing software—MS Word, Notes—have inbuilt templates. In addition, some of these templates are available online too.
- It is advisable to use a font size of at least 11. You should appreciate that your reviewer might not have the vision of Spiderman.
- Most common fonts used to make resumes are Times New Roman, Calibri or Arial.
- The text is typed in black colour. Avoid loud shades of pink while drafting a resume.
- All points should be left aligned with a margin of 0.5 inches on all four sides.
- It is best to avoid white spaces while framing sentences; most points should occupy more than half a line.

- Finally, running spellcheck is a must. The last thing you need is a resume with spelling mistakes

Content Is King and Rightly So

The core of any resume is the content in it. Following are some key points that should be considered while designing content.

- The first line of each section should highlight the impact of that section. It is advisable to highlight benefits in the aggregate form. For instance, 'led a team of x people', 'generated y savings', 'won x competitions', 'secured x national ranks'.
- Each subsequent line should highlight a set of words to drive across a point. In case you are interviewing for a job with specific skills, mention those words explicitly and highlight them. For aspiring B-school students, they might like to highlight points around 'analytics', 'client facing', 'certifications', 'club leadership' and so on.
- The ordering of points in a section should be in a decreasing order of impact. Most recruiters end up reading, at best, only the first two lines in any section.
- While sending out a resume, some recruiters or business schools ask for references. It is important to attach these. Needless to say, they have to be appropriately informed in advance.

The trickiest part in making a resume is often what comes after it. A good resume often leads to an interview. At the interview, it is important that the candidate is fully prepared on every line mentioned in his resume. An ideal way is to have rehearsed content for a couple of minutes on each line mentioned in the resume. In case of academic projects or work experience, the candidate can speak about his/her role followed by what he or she did and the impact they had.

One of the most common interview questions is, 'Tell me something about yourself that is not in the resume?' It is advisable to keep a couple of points (e.g., interesting travel experiences, hobbies, special interests) not mentioned in the resume as potential talking points.

In conclusion, making a resume is part art and part science. Like most things in life, making it for the first time can seem tedious and boring. In addition to following the principles mentioned above, it is always advisable to show your draft resume to seniors, parents, college counsellors or someone at work for their qualified opinion. Finally, a good resume serves the role of a good book cover. It should be remembered that in this case, 'all that glitters is actually gold!'

50

EXCELLING IN A GROUP DISCUSSION

The group discussion stage is the second stage in most business school admission processes in India. Although its weightage in the overall process is relatively lower than the written exam and the personal interview, the round can prove to be tricky at times. In addition, the group discussion round is a key stage for being selected in leading corporate houses.[71]

While a strong performance in this round doesn't guarantee a selection but a poor performance can go a long way in rejecting the candidature. This chapter focuses on the skills that are tested as part of this round and how candidates can be best prepared to ace this round.

There are certain important skills that are tested for an aspiring management professional as part of the group discussion stage. The primary skill that is tested is his/her ability to communicate crisply and freely. Such a skill is paramount in future negotiations or discussions in a candidate's corporate career. In addition, a key skill that is tested is also about the candidate's ability to work with others in a group and how well they build on others' viewpoints.

Aspiring management professionals can look at the following avenues to be best prepared for this round. Most topics given during this round revolve around current affairs. Candidates should read the newspapers and business magazines thoroughly over the last few months. For candidates, a critical skill to be practised is argument construction. The standard framework for argument construction is to start with the argument ('I think A is good for the economy') followed with the reason ('A is good as it leads to an increase in B and C') followed with the evidence ('e.g., in the past, data points D and E prove it').

There are some obvious tips that candidates can follow to improve their chances at this stage:

- **Never be selfish:** It is advisable to not come across as selfish in the discussion. Nobody likes a candidate who keeps talking endlessly. It is best to ensure that all points are made in not more than 30 seconds.
- **Simplify:** It is best to speak in simple sentences without unnecessary qualifiers and adverbs. All points to be made can follow the Argument, Reason and Evidence construct.
- **Summarize:** A few minutes into the discussion, it is a smart tactic to summarize where the group stands on the points made in the discussion. If pulled off well with most points accommodated, a natural leadership flair is on display about the candidate.
- **Avoid extreme opinions:** Irrespective of what a candidate's personal opinions are, it is not recommended that a candidate takes extreme positions in a discussion (e.g., Mr ABC sucks, I hate XYZ). It should also be remembered that the panellists will ask you follow up questions on your opinions in the personal interview round.
- **Avoid incorrect statements:** Needless to say, socially and politically incorrect statements have to be avoided (e.g., women should take care of home because it is their primary responsibility)

Despite your best preparation, your group discussion can go completely haywire in case you have a 'noise polluter' or a 'jackass' in the panel as one of the other candidates. A 'noise polluter' keeps on talking, ranting along without allowing anyone else to speak. The following are some pointers on how to handle a noise polluter:

- A noise polluter will incorrigibly interrupt when you speak. In such a scenario, it is best to assertively comment, 'Give me 10 more seconds please. Let me finish my point'.

- A noise polluter will often alienate everyone as everyone will dislike him instantly. In such a case, it is best to form implicit alliances with other members in the panel. It is a smart move to 'agree' to others and 'building on their lines of reasoning'. Often, the other person will return the favour and will start favouring you.

- If things go completely south with the 'noise polluter' rampaging along, it may be necessary to resort to tough language along lines of 'let others make their point, your point has been made, let us hear another point of view'.

In conclusion, although the group discussion process is a lesser weightage round in the business school admission or corporate job placement process, it can prove to be very tricky as a strong performance doesn't guarantee a selection but a poor performance almost assures a rejection. Irrespective of the process, mastering the skills in a group discussion go a long way in driving corporate success.

51

THE SLOG OVERS

Sudhir Singh, an IIM aspirant, has been preparing for the CAT for close to a year. As his D-day approaches, he is unsure of his course of action. Should he go full throttle in the last few days or take it a little easy?

The Common Admission Test (CAT) is one of the most important examinations in an aspiring management professional's life as it provides access to the hallowed portals of an IIM. Given the high stakes and the immense competition involved, candidates spend a lot of time, sometimes in years, preparing for this exam. More often than not, the last few weeks before the big day are supremely critical. During this phase, it is important to strike the right blend between excessive rigour and adequate rest.

Avoid Learning Anything New

Unlike routine school and college exams, in which bulk of the preparation is done a few hours before the exam, the CAT works in a very different way. The CAT is a specialized exam which needs months of practice. In such a case, it is highly recommended that nothing new is learnt a few days before. Mastering any new concept takes weeks of practice and is best recommended to be kept out of the candidate's gambit during the last few days. Moreover, newer concepts and themes can prove to be overwhelming and demoralizing at the last minute.

As an extension, during the last few days, crash courses and concentrated group studies can create more harm than good. It is always best to spread out a preparation rather than cram it a week before.

Be Choosy while Reading Online Forums

There are numerous forums (e.g., PaGaLGuY, chat rooms offered by coaching institutes) in which candidates discuss aspects about the exam and its associated elements. Needless to say, these forums are extremely useful as candidates discuss exam patterns, questions, tips from faculty and past students. While it is a very good idea to be an active part of these groups, participating in these discussion groups a few weeks before the exam can be tricky. There are numerous characters who deliberately spread panic on these forums days before the exam by overwhelming participants with rumours and possible formats about the exam.

Always Advisable to Re-do Past Question Papers

It is best to re-do mock question papers, set by coaching centres, during this phase. Each mock question paper is unique and enables candidates to learn new concepts. Re-doing these papers can help in refreshing key concepts. In addition, re-doing past years' CAT papers is always helpful. The IIMs also release a mock exam paper, it is advisable to go through this thoroughly.

By now, the candidate should also be clear about his/her areas of strength and weakness. For instance, in quantitative aptitude, a candidate can be clear about his/her area of strength (e.g., geometry) and area of possible weakness (e.g., probability). On the D-day, solving questions starting from the area of strength is always advisable.

Lead a Monk-Like Life during the Last Two Days

The last day or two before the D-day is extremely critical. It is best to sleep well during the last few days. Needless to say, there should be little or no entertainment. Late nights and heavy cramming are not recommended. Unnecessary physical activity during the last two days should also be avoided. It is best to stay at home, eat regular food, read a little (unrelated to the exam) and sleep well before the D-day.

In conclusion, the CAT exam is often a game changer for thousands of aspiring management professionals. However, what should also be remembered is that it is just another exam with candidates getting multiple attempts at it. Candidates should remember this and treat it accordingly.

Sudhir decides to go easy over the last few days relying on a few cursory glances at the mock CAT papers he attempted earlier.

52 | CONSTRUCTING A HIGH-PROFILE LINKEDIN PAGE

A high-profile LinkedIn page is a great reflection of individual talent and professional achievement. Given most of us are business school graduates, our LinkedIn page is analogous to what an Instagram page is to a cinematic professional. Authoring your own high-impact LinkedIn page used to be fairly easy, throw in a combination of 'accomplished', 'designed', 'led', 'initiated', 'achieved' and similar metaphors. If you were really good, you would garnish your page with a 'design thinker' or a 'customer experience architect'. However, with most things in life, composing a high-profile LinkedIn page has come a long way. This chapter highlights this evolution.[72]

My Middle Name Is Cryptic

Any modern-day LinkedIn page begins with a technological flavour. Even if your digital literary is at best limited to making pivot tables, throw in a 'digital evangelist' in your write up. If you managed to read a Wikipedia page on crypto-currency, you are qualified to add 'crypto enthusiast'. If you happened to study BASIC (Beginner's All Purpose Symbolic Instruction Code) programming language in Class 6 in school, the world will adore you if you add 'blockchain enthusiast'.

Nothing Makes the World Go around Like Leadership

At business school, most graduates are taught to pursue leadership for reaching business *moksha* (enlightenment).

This endearing spirit is what your LinkedIn page should reflect in abundance. Throw in a 'life coach' given you must be playing 'agony aunt' to most depressed millennials. In addition, if you own even one share in any company, you can garnish your page with a 'value investor', 'contrarian investor', 'board member' or 'CXO advisor'. If you are really high on yourself, try pushing your limits with a 'venture capitalist' or a 'transformation champion'.

All of a Sudden, Everything Is about Family

In contemporary social media, family is making a comeback in acquiring a 'cool quotient'. So it is fairly obvious it has to reflect on our LinkedIn pages. The world will celebrate with great gusto if you can add a tinge of 'father', 'mother', 'husband', 'wife', 'friend' to your LinkedIn page. People have to realize that being a family member in this decade is so much more difficult than the thousands of years gone by.

In Michael Jackson's Words, 'Make the World a Better Place'

After family, making the world a better place has become very sexy. A one-rupee donation to a beggar can earn you a tag of a 'philanthropist'. Given the biggest curse of our generation is unrelenting depression, a 'happiness coach' or a 'motivational speaker' is bound to earn you brownie points with the opposite sex. Diversity is the new correct in business discourse, playfully decorate your page with a 'diversity advocate' to seamlessly fit in.

Follow Your Passion and You Will Never Have to Work a Day in Your Life

Being passionate about something is the 'in thing' of our generation. To live up to this ideal, your LinkedIn page should witness you wearing your passion on your sleeve. Throw in a 'wildlife photographer' even if all you have managed to do is click the domesticated cockroach. If you have a minimum of five friends on Facebook or Instagram, you qualify to be a 'social media influencer'. If you are the intellectual type, you can try the philosophy of 'Ted Attendee' or 'Ted Advocate'. If you ever borrowed money from a friend and never returned it, a 'serial entrepreneur' tag will drape your entire profile page with unending passion.

While it is fairly obvious what is trending on LinkedIn today, let me take a leap of faith and suggest what will be trending on LinkedIn a few years down the line. I see the following dominating the professional discourse, 'love angel', 'policy advocate', 'social engineering champion', 'thinker', 'status quo disrupter'. I am happy to hear your thoughts only if you agree with me!

In conclusion, a man's chest is measured by the attractiveness of his LinkedIn page. With the above guiding principles, it is not very difficult to build an artificially attractive and professionally trending chest.

53

THE LURE OF THE INTERNATIONAL MBA

Rounak Sethi, an engineer from IIT Kanpur, had interview calls from all major IIMs. He ended up converting most of them but chose not to join any. His friends look at him in disbelief as he lets go an IIM Ahmedabad seat. He is keen on studying in an Ivy League college. Neither is he the department rank 1 nor is he the student council president. He is somewhere in the middle. His is not an isolated trend.[73]

Over the last few years, an increasing number of Indian students are flocking to top business schools worldwide. In fact, Indian students are one of the largest nationalities in any of the top international business schools. The *crème de la crème* from the best Indian institutions are choosing to head to the west rather than study at the hallowed portals of the IIMs. This chapter looks at this emerging trend.

The glamour of doing an MBA from the IIMs has remained stagnant at best.

A decade ago, doing an MBA from an IIM was paramount to being conferred with celebrity status. From superior matrimonial prospects to newspaper interviews to being worshipped in your residential colonies, life almost changed overnight.

Over the last few years, the sheen of an MBA from IIM has worn off. Possible reasons that could have contributed to this could be the rapid increase in the number of IIMs and a significant increase in the average batch size. At present, there are 20 IIMs with few more in the pipeline. Average batch size at the bigger IIMs has crossed 450.

Post the economic downturn, the plush banking jobs from the London and New York desks have steadily declined. It hasn't helped that after so many years there are only two to three IIMs in the *Financial Times* Top 100 B-schools.

Global exposure and better financing schemes have resulted in increased attractiveness of the international MBA from a top business school.

With senior management roles becoming geography agnostic, an international role or an international education has almost become mandatory. As a result, young MBA aspirants are looking positively at an international MBA from a top business school.

The experience offered at an international school in terms of diversity, study treks, alumni network is unmatchable. For instance, at London Business School, there are students from more than 80 countries in a batch. Any international MBA has typical study treks in countries like Turkey, China, South Africa, Germany, Hong Kong and so on. Students at INSEAD can study at three campuses the world over—Fontainebleau, Singapore and Abu Dhabi. The alumni network at these institutions is unparalleled with representations from more than 100 countries.

The cost of an international MBA has remained steep. Students can expect to pay at least $120,000 to complete a two-year MBA at a top-ranked school like Harvard or Stanford. However, universities are looking to increase affordability by offering graduate assistantship opportunities, easy loans and alternate sources of income. Even then, it nearly takes three years to pay back a loan for an international MBA.

However, over the last few years, the cost of an MBA from India has increased steadily. For instance, the cost of an MBA at the Indian School of Business is nearly ₹30 lakhs with the top IIMs costing nearly 25 lakhs.

Importance of diversity, ROI and preferred work location are key parameters to choose between an Indian and an international MBA.

There is a clear case to do an MBA from an IIM. Especially if an aspirant wants to work and settle in India. No institute can promise a better starting point. The ROI, in pure financial terms, is significantly more lucrative than an international MBA. More often than not, engineers who don't want to be in software technology use the IIM route to choose another career path.

An MBA from a Top 10 international business school has a clear-cut case in its favour. Global outlook, exceptional alumni network, incredible diversity, global roles being some of the few benefits. If an aspirant wants to work outside India for a few years, a Top 10 international business school is an extremely attractive proposition. The salary increase after an MBA is equally high. For instance, MBA candidates at London Business School reported a 107 per cent increase in their salaries after their MBA.

However, if a candidate fails to secure a Top 10 business school, the decision to choose between an IIM and a global business school borders on shades of grey. International business schools often don't have a 100 per cent placement track record. The prospect of not landing a high paying job in a shaky economy with a ridiculously high loan can be extremely challenging for an MBA candidate. Needless to say, it is getting more difficult to secure work visas in the UK and the United States.

Many IIM graduates are pursuing their second MBA at top international business schools.

Over the last few years, an increasing number of IIM graduates are pursuing their second MBA at top business schools worldwide. The traditional MBA program in India is largely directed towards individuals with a few years of work experience. More and more graduates are doing the second MBA at top business schools to give their careers an international boost, change their industry or geography or to avoid stagnation in their present jobs.

A Top 10 International Business School Is a No-brainer

In conclusion, studying in a Top 10 business school is an experience of a lifetime. The entire package, comprising unbelievable diversity, incredible alumni and global job opportunities, can't be matched by any Indian business school. However, the choice becomes tricky when the candidate has to choose between an institute not in the Top 10 and an IIM.

Rounak has a final admission call from Columbia business school. Although he has been rejected by Harvard and Stanford, he decides to study in Columbia amidst the hustle and bustle of New York City!

Is That So?

1. Did you know that only 2 per cent of students at Harvard have flunked out?
2. Did you know that the phrase 'Ivy League' is believed to have been coined by a sportswriter at the New York Tribune who used it disparagingly for Princeton and Columbia's football teams?
3. Did you know that INSEAD's class of 2019 contains representatives from over 70 countries?
4. Did you know that the first IIT (Kharagpur) and the first IIM (Calcutta) were set-up in West Bengal?

54

NAILING YOUR INTERNSHIP

Arpit Agarwal, an MBA from IIM Lucknow, after numerous interviews landed a plum international summer internship with the New York office of a leading investment bank. A ridiculously high stipend combined with an accommodation in Manhattan, Arpit is keen to put in the long hours to do well. How can Arpit look at creating maximum impact during his eight-week internship?[74]

The summer internship, an 8–10 week program at the end of the first year often gives Indian MBA graduates their first exposure to corporate life. Over the last few years, the summer internship is becoming increasingly important as corporates are looking at the internship route to make full-time offers. Companies, more often than not, have realistic but challenging expectations from their summer interns. Although sometimes intimidating, there are a few guiding principles an intern can follow to create maximum impact during this period.

The summer internship, an 8–10 week program at the end of the first year of an MBA, is a good starting point, for most graduates, of their corporate careers.

Recruitment for the summer internship program occurs during the much-hyped summer placements at business schools. Typical recruiters include management consulting firms (e.g., McKinsey & Company, Boston Consulting Group, Bain & Company), investment banks (e.g., Morgan Stanley, Deutsche Bank, Edelweiss), FMCG firms (e.g., HUL, Procter and Gamble, Nestle) and general management firms (e.g., Tata Administrative Services, Aditya Birla Group). Over the last few years, leading business schools have seen a huge influx of e-commerce recruiters (e.g., Flipkart, Snapdeal, Amazon).

For most Indian MBA graduates, the summer internship is their first exposure to corporate life. The internship serves as an important exercise in directionally guiding them about the career of their choice. The stipends offered during internships are quite attractive. Leading investment banks and consulting firms offer between ₹100,000 a month and ₹400,000 a month depending on the location of the internship while leading FMCG firms offer a stipend of ₹75,000 a month to ₹150,000 a month.

Over the last few years, companies are increasingly looking at the summer internship route to make full-time offers.

'About 60 per cent associates of the 2013 batch at Citi were hired through the summer internship channel,' says Anuranjita Kumar, Country HR Officer, Citi India.

'We save at least 200 man days if we take more management graduates through the PPO route,' says Prince Augustin, Executive Vice President, Group Human Capital and Leadership Development, Mahindra & Mahindra.

The internship serves as a win-win proposition for both the recruiter and the intern. The recruiter gets to look at an intern for a period of eight weeks, instead of a few interviews, before deciding to make a full-time offer. The intern gets to experience the industry first hand before saying yes to the recruiter.

In all likelihood, the intern serves as an odd job man on the team. However, there is opportunity to create impact in any piece of work assigned.

The intern, rarely, has the ownership of a complete module. He or she often assists a team member in their work or is the secondary owner of a module. He or she is the typical odd job boy carrying out ad hoc data analysis, carrying out a few customer interviews, making a few backup slides, spending inordinate hours googling and so on.

It is but natural that an intern, being new to that profession, will not be given a critical piece of work. However, even in seemingly inconsequential jobs, substantial impact can be created. FMCG companies in India are flooded with examples of new product launches that were a result of an insight that emerged from an intern's interview with customers.

The recruiter rarely evaluates an intern on subject knowledge. Learning curve and attitude often play a key role in deciding whether the recruiter makes a full-time offer or not.

The intern is not expected to be the expert in that sector. In fact, he or she is not expected to know anything about the sector. However, he or she is expected to grasp and pick up things quickly. The intern can look at reading his recruiter's annual reports or setting up news alerts of his recruiter or clients or his industry. Regularly passing on the latest industry items to his team members will be well appreciated.

In terms of skills, the intern is not expected to be an excel whiz kid. He or she is expected to be proficient with basic Microsoft Excel or PowerPoint. The rest is to be picked up on the job.

Key personality traits that are well appreciated during an internship include readiness to take on jobs which border on monotony or laborious and the attitude to learn irrespective of the type of module the intern is working on. An intern can always add value no matter what the situation. Even a simple exercise like taking notes and following up on action items in a meeting where he or she had no role to play can be a useful activity.

To be better acclimatized during the internship, an intern can choose the right set of electives during the term before the internship. Investment banking interns will benefit by choosing electives in the areas of Financial Derivatives and

Corporate Finance. FMCG interns will benefit by choosing electives in the areas of Consumer Behaviour and Sales & Distribution Management. Interns across fields will benefit by opting for an elective in Spreadsheet Modelling.

Reluctance to experiment and grow during the internship can put off your recruiter and be fatal to the intern's chances of getting a full-time offer.

An intern might be a 'rockstar' at his business school. But an 'I know it all' attitude rarely impresses people at the workplace. Especially for a greenhorn who has little idea about the nuts and bolts about that industry. An intern should never be afraid to ask for help when the work is getting over demanding. Not asking for help and turning in incorrect work later on can crucify his chances.

It can be nearly suicidal for an intern to stick only to his team members. Networking with other people in the corporate is always beneficial. Recruiters often organize multiple events (e.g., plays, visits to a resort, visits to IPL matches, etc) for interns to network and get to know other people at the firm.

Needless to say, basic corporate etiquette errors should be avoided. It doesn't make sense for an intern to Facebook or Twitter all day if he or she doesn't have work. In such a case, voluntarily asking for work can help. Basic grooming is a given. Turning up in hippie clothing or dressed as a Christmas tree is a strict no-no.

In conclusion, the internship is the beginning to a career of two decades ahead. If it goes well, it can result in a full-time offer from a leading recruiter giving the intern a good start. Unfortunately, that is all it is—a good start.

Hence, it is important to focus on the summer internship but not treat it as the panache to all problems in life.

In a nutshell, it is equivalent to going 2–0 in the first set in a five-set clash. In fact, life after business school might or might not be so rosy. The next chapter shows you the mirror to your future.

Arpit, during his eight weeks, plans to make full use of his weekends and enjoy the sights and sounds of New York, Boston, Atlantic City and a trip to Los Angeles before he returns home. Not a bad choice for a 23-year-old.

Is That So?

1. Did you know that some investment banks (e.g., Deutsche Bank) offer summer interns the opportunity to work across two desks across two countries in a span of two months?
2. Did you know that some business schools (e.g., NITIE) in India have a winter internship in addition to a summer internship to facilitate greater industry exposure for their students?
3. Did you know that many business schools (e.g., IIM Ahmedabad, IIM Bangalore, IIM Calcutta) have an industry interface club as part of which students can undertake live industry projects in their second year of MBA?

55

IMMEDIATE LIFE AFTER A BUSINESS SCHOOL

Raghav Sood, a fresh marketing business graduate from IIM Calcutta, always aspired to be a hot shot brand manager. Meeting Ogilvy in the morning, designing a brilliant ad campaign in the afternoon and shooting an advertisement with Katrina Kaif a couple of days later. Needless to say, a flat in Bandra West, a couple of young achiever awards and an interview to India's biggest business magazine would follow. As he gets ready to interview the next Sarpanch in Deoria village on the outskirts of Gorakhpur in Uttar Pradesh amidst the 47-degree heat, he wonders what happened to his dreams.[75]

Management education is one of the most hyped streams in India. Due to the incessant press coverage and unrelenting pressures, fresh MBA graduates are expected to sit on a pedestal immediately after passing out of business school. Unrealistic expectations are also compounded by the fact that substantial MBA graduates are freshers who have not witnessed corporate life before. Reality, however, is not so hunky dory as everyone has to go through the grind. This chapter looks at what new recruits after business school face in their first year, how they can effectively manage their expectations and make the most out of it.

The first year at work encourages fresh recruits to be the 'jack of all trades'.

Across companies, fresh MBA graduates are generally part of a management trainee program. In FMCG companies (e.g., Hindustan Unilever, P&G, Marico, Dabur), the management trainee program has a duration of 12–18 months and involves stints across rural sales, urban sales, marketing, manufacturing and an international location. New hires are given limited responsibility and expected to excel in that limited role. General management companies (e.g., Aditya Birla Group, Tata Administrative Services) have similar programs for young recruits. Fresh graduates work in different group companies before being assigned their eventual position depending on the firm's requirements and the individual preferences. Roles at corporate banking profiles (e.g., Standard Chartered, Rabo, ICICI) involve multiple stints across departments/desks/countries before settling into one final role. Similar is the story at investment banking firms. Management consulting firms, however, do not have such a management trainee program. New recruits are staffed on client-facing cases straightaway. The new recruit is primarily responsible to undertake hours of googling and secondary research to extract all data available.

Reality is often harsh especially when viewed through rose-tinted sunglasses. Everyone, absolutely everyone, has to go through the grind.

Fresh recruits after business school are often disappointed during their first year at work. The core reason being disproportionate mismatch between their expectations and reality. Fresh graduates often expect a five-star lifestyle along with fame and power inside their new organization. Their expectations of a five-star lifestyle often meet a dead end with brick and mortar recruiters making a deliberate attempt to make them sensitive to real India, by making them stay in rural India for months or making them stay in hotels with daily tariff less than ₹1000/day.

The bigger point is that they are no longer the poster boys of their sections or clubs or project groups. They work with many senior people in a department or on a project where

IMMEDIATE LIFE AFTER A BUSINESS SCHOOL

their greatest contribution is not to make any major goof up. They end up doing dry, boring, uninteresting work day in and day out through the first year. The 'resume point mindset' which they acquired in business school can be a source of great dissonance.

Although expected, work hours are long across the board. Corporates make fresh recruits spend longer hours doing the drudgery. More often than not, their work is often not required or is considered irrelevant to the organization.

Although performance is stressed upon, the first-year achievements are not fretted upon heavily by recruiters.

The first year is counted as an investment by corporates, they don't expect much in return.

Most corporates don't expect a new recruit to know or contribute other than their basic business knowledge acquired at business school. New recruits are expected to learn the nuts and bolts of business and do whatever job, however dry, exceedingly well. In some cases, especially FMCG firms, physical hardship (e.g., bad postings, horrible accommodation, unreasonable bosses) are deliberately enforced upon management trainees to test their character and to build in them appreciation for the lower rung workforce.

Management trainees or fresh business graduates should look to leverage upon their resources to the maximum. Regular interaction with the allocated mentor on areas like their career interest, discussions on challenges faced by them will help to a great extent. Networking, as always, across departments will hold fresh recruits in great stead. Finally, they should learn to create a perceived impact, even with their limited responsibility, in the organization. Creating a perceived impact is the single biggest quality they should imbibe.

In conclusion, the first year after an MBA can be quite tricky. While reality can be disheartening for lofty eyed business graduates, there is a sound reason for them to get acquainted with the dry boring work at the bottom of the pyramid. The first year serves as an excellent opportunity for business graduates to learn the nuts and bolts of business. The sunny side is that the pressure to perform in the first year is limited allowing a fresh business graduate to settle in and experiment comfortably.

Raghav doesn't lose hope. He realises that interviewing the Sarpanch is a critical part of the learning curve before shooting the advertisement with Katrina Kaif.

Is That So?

1. Did you know that the management trainee program at TAS (Tata Administrative Services) is one of the most coveted general management programs across companies?
2. Did you know that most management trainee programs at FMCG firms involve one international stint?
3. Did you know that corporates have started paying hefty joining bonuses to attract and retain fresh recruits from business school?
4. Did you know that ~25–30 per cent of fresh business school graduates shift jobs during their first two years after business school?

56 | SELF-SABOTAGING SOCIAL MEDIA HABITS

Mehak Jaiswal, a young competent MBA from IIM Ahmedabad is a hardcore social media addict. As a teenager, she has grown up on Instagram, Facebook and Twitter. She pledges to continue her social media addiction along with TikTok on her first day at work. She tries to verbalize the most important rules which she plans to earnestly follow over the next few months to make a positive impact at her place of work.[76]

Thou Shall Follow Your Boss, Their Boss and All Their Pretty Spouses on Instagram

In a globalized, 24×7 connected world, Instagram is a brilliant platform to connect with your boss, your boss' boss, your client lead, your peers and so on. The office is after all one big family. Everyone deserves to know the fun side of everyone else.

With one glamorous picture of your latest polka-dotted pink shirt, they can understand how privileged they are to work with you. Now that they are following you, they can appreciate pictures of your dog, your date, your culinary skills, your photography skills, your soulful blog and so on. They will be delighted at the amount of free time you have every day. And you shouldn't complain with the liberal dosage of weekend work you get after that.

In professional working spaces, it is highly recommended to avoid staying connected to your boss, his boss and his pretty wife on Instagram and Facebook.

Thou Shall Stalk Your Pretty Colleagues and Their Spouses on LinkedIn and Twitter

With the onslaught of social media over the last decade, everyone understands that personal lives are no longer personal. A young graduate can get more insight into a senior leader's personality by stalking him/his pretty spouse on LinkedIn and Instagram. Thanks to LinkedIn premium membership, senior leaders will even come to know who is stalking their spouse online. They will appreciate the genuine interest you have taken in their personal life.

Needless to say, it is never a good idea to come across as a stalker on social media. Do you have second thoughts about this?

Thou Shall Keep the World Updated about You, One Post an Hour about Your Brushing, Pooping, Dining and Dating Regimen

It is so difficult to be in touch with everyone and communicate your inner beauty to the rest of the world these days. Thanks to Instagram and TikTok, everybody can be updated on your football team's strengths, your latest date, your Ola cab bill, which 5-star hotel you had dinner in. It is only natural for your bosses to admire the time you spend on social media during office hours. The admiration is only natural and will not result in any extra work.

Again, as mentioned earlier, it is sensible to keep social media accounts private and circulated with only a close circle of friends. Trying to make your boss jealous with your page 3 lifestyle is never a good idea.

Thou Shall Bitch about Your Client or Your Boss or a Bad Timeline on Your Social Media Page

All of us have bad days. From the monster of a boss, the devil incarnates in terms of the client or the sadistic timeline everyone has to put up with. Social media is a natural platform to vent out a bit of frustration to make your life significantly better. Everyone will appreciate your sentiment if you post about your increment being lower than inflation or if your boss is deliberately trying to spend more time with you on weekends. Given the power of the internet, word will spread to a wider audience.

Even people, who are not on your friends list, deserve to know about the devil in your life. Given that Twitter sometimes picks up your Facebook posts automatically, your boss will become a more reasonable man once he has realized all your frustrations aired in public.

As our grandmothers used to advise us to never wash dirty linen in public, it is a terrible idea to make an unfavourable reference about your client, boss or company on social media. Even if you have another job and are trying to get your current company to release you early!

Thou Shall Post a Selfie with Everyone You Meet in Office

As part of the Yuppie generation, a selfie is equivalent to oxygen for survival. It is normal to put up a selfie with anyone who has made a positive or a negative impact on your life. Your Managing Director would love to be clicked with you in an 'awww' selfie that generates more than 2,500 likes. Post the success of the first 'awww' selfie, all the other managing directors will queue up outside your cubicle to be a part of more 'awww' selfies.

No guidance needed on this point, I am sure you have got the gist of it by now.

Thou Shall Put Up Pictures of You Swimming Like a Mermaid in Bali

God has been immensely kind to you by giving you the physique of a mermaid. In addition, you have worked incredibly hard to replicate the toned abs of Ileana D' Cruz. It is only natural that the world witness your pictures of dancing on the beach or swimming like a mermaid in Bali. Given that some people, including your bosses, might be upset over their excessive work and cancelled vacations, they will be delighted to 'like' your photograph in a figure-hugging swimsuit. After all, they couldn't enjoy life as a greenhorn. At least they will take solace in the fact that the next generation is.

Again, you shouldn't stay connected on social media with your bosses. Neither do you want to be burdened with useless work nor do you want the attention of pot-bellied middle-aged men salivating over your pictures.

Thou Shall Regularly Rant about Certain Races Regularly

There are few things that are cool to post on social media these days.

MS Dhoni is past his prime. Reforms have got stalled. Govinda's yellow trousers are cute. Beetroot is everyone's favourite dish. You are preparing for the 21 km Mumbai Marathon. Add to that the 'uribaba' Bong, the uncouth Haryanvi Jat and the overweight Gujju!

If you are from Delhi, the 'Madrasis' have always been an object of ridicule. It makes sense to post about their accent, their 'sambhar' and Rajnikanth. Your next boss, who will be a 'Madrasi', will be considerate and try to change his race's behaviour.

Political correctness is extremely important in modern contemporary careers. Avoid all forms of political, racist or any form of derogatory comments.

Thou Shall Definitely Post on Social Media when Drunk or Smashed

Everybody is supremely honest while drunk or high. It is but natural that your friends would want to know what you really think of them when you are high. A friend of mine put up a video of him trying to ride a dog at a beach in Goa. The uploaded video went viral and generated a ridiculous number of views. His bosses, who might have missed out on the finance minister's budget speech, made it a point to watch his video and appreciate his dog riding capabilities.

Do you want your boss to see your video of riding a dog in Goa? Or worse?

Better Safe than Sorry When It Comes to Recommended Social Media Etiquette

Corporate success for young MBA graduates is often a function of their brand image and perception in their firm. Provocative, racial or insensitive content, when read by peers or senior leaders, can alter a favourable perception of an MBA graduate in their minds. The golden rule is to assume that the entire world might be reading what you are going to put up.

It is advisable to keep all professional contacts, especially bosses, clients and senior leaders, away from an MBA graduate's Instagram or Facebook page. It is also sensible to delay the announcements of all the good things in life on a graduate's social media page, a fancy holiday, a reduction in waist size, a new office or a new job till you settle in. Avoid stereotyping and abusing your client/boss/company/government/men/women publicly.

In fact, it makes sense to google your name and take down any negative content that might appear in your name. Finally, it is important to be abreast about your company's social media policy. Not complying with such a policy can prove to be disastrous.

In conclusion, it is important to be conscious of what you are putting on your social media pages. A harmless post can go a long way in creating an unfavourable opinion in the minds of senior corporate leaders. In one sentence, not everything in life is about getting 500 likes per post or a picture.

If I put up this chapter on my Facebook page, I am not sure if it will get 500 views/likes. It might even be irritating to my friends. In fact, it might be violating one of the principles I earlier spoke about.

But then, Mehak is far more irritating than I am. If the world can tolerate her, I am an absolute cakewalk.

Is That So?

1. Did you know that some babies have been named Facebook in Egypt?
2. Did you know that the limit on the number of friends in Facebook is 5,000?
3. Did you know that LinkedIn is used by 95 per cent of companies who employ social media for hiring people?
4. Did you know that 'Selfies at Funerals' and 'Selfies with Homeless People' went viral over the last few months?

HAPPINESS

LONGING FOR A MEANINGFUL LIFE

Finally, it is not easy being us, millennials. The constant pressure of expectations from family and society, the boredom due to meaningless work, the relentless need to keep up our Instagram page and living with the 'fake it till you make it psychology', the sedentary lifestyles, hollow relationships, poor social friendships, massive financial debt and finding a true connection with life can bring down any strong minded and intelligent person. This section, in my opinion, is the most important one in the book and has by design been addressed at the end.

66

Never laugh at your wife's choices.
You are one of them.
Unknown

The problem with the rat race is that even
if you win, you're still a rat.
Lilly Tomlin
American actress and comedian

99

57

WHY SHOULD YOU READ BUSINESS BOOKS?

When I anchored the Bangalore Business Literature Festival last year, one of our chief guests, my old professor from IIM Bangalore mentioned how she used to consciously measure her change in beliefs and outlook to life by looking at her reading shelf over the last few months. It seemed an interesting concept to measure your personal evolution by looking at the books read over a period of time. In case you are an avid reader, you should track your reading shelf over the last few months. In case you aren't, this is the time to build a reading shelf.

As cliché as it might sound, developing a strong reading habit is necessary to continuously learn and improve your professional competence. Globally, most CEOs are known to be voracious readers. Reading 52 books a year is no longer a passing fad but endorsed by many business leaders. Given we are millennials and understand goals, a business book a month is a sound goal to start with. To manipulate your mind in a positive way, Instagram the book cover you are going to read and put a short note at the end of your reading journey on what you liked about the book. This habit works like magic to push you to read more. In chemical terms, you are using the dopamine generation to your advantage.

To assist you in this journey, I have put together a list of books you can start off with. Yes, you are welcome![77]

The Intelligent Investor by Benjamin Graham

The bible of financial investing *The Intelligent Investor* introduced practical investing to millions of readers. It speaks of value or emotionless investing based on hard work, patience and discipline over a period of time. In my personal opinion, this book is akin to the Bhagavad Gita. Every time you read it, you learn an incredible amount. The first time I read the book was in 2010 and thought the contents of the book were obvious and common sensical. I read the book again in 2018 after having made every mistake the book warned me against.

Good Boss, Bad Boss by Robert Sutton

Everyone relates to a book about a bad boss, irrespective of industry, country, gender or race. *Good Boss, Bad Boss* is based on several emails and calls the author received from innocent civilians ranting about their incorrigible bosses. Written in an inimitable sarcastic style, the book is bound to connect and bring a smile to anyone who has worked in a corporate. A piece of caution though, you shouldn't end up gifting a copy of the book to your sub-ordinate or your boss.

The Billionaire's Apprentice by Anita Raghavan

I am convinced that *The Billionaire's Apprentice* is bound to be converted into a movie someday. Revolving around the insider trading case of Sri Lankan billionaire Raj Rajaratnam and ex-McKinsey head Rajat Gupta, the book is a thrilling amalgamation of greed, emotion, fame and a crime thriller on the chase of the allegedly crooked by the FBI. The book chronicles the sensational rise and fall of Rajat Gupta alongside portraying a balanced picture of the events that shook up his awe inspiring kingdom. A worthy read into the world of the high flying, not so scrupulous, money minting machines. Given that most of you will enter the high-profile services industry, this book is highly recommended.

Why I Left Goldman Sachs by Greg Smith

The book that will actually end up becoming a movie is *Why I Left Goldman Sachs*. It chronicles the journey of a 21-year-old from an idealistic intern at Goldman Sachs to a leadership position after battling the lure of the greenback, surviving in a winner takes all mentality, overcoming a terrifying recession, managing conflicts of interest after duping iconic American companies and rigging the financial system in which there is only one possible winner. The inherent lifestyle of the industry is also well captured in the Leonardo DiCaprio starrer *The Wolf of Wall Street!*

Satan's Angels by Sandeep Das

Although it might be surprising, I did end up reading my own book again over the last year. *Satan's Angels* is a business fiction chronicling the perils of private equity-owned business conglomerates in a post liberalized India. It depicts a sensational journey of greed, filth, glamour, success, rage and jealousy across a gamut of continents, industries and dozens of characters. By design, the book is intended to be a plate of biryani among hungry college students—meant to be finished at a go!

The Next 100 Years by George Friedman

The Next 100 Years is a fascinating book on the likely turnouts of countries and political alliances in the next century. The author, a foreign policy expert, makes daring predictions about the future from the continued domination of the United States, the rise of Mexico, the breakup of China to the potential of a Third World War fought in space.

Although the book focuses on the political ramifications in the future, the implications to business are worth a read. Sample this, the author forecasts that the American economy and by extension its stock markets, will lead the world for many decades to come. So you might want to hold on to your shares of the NASDAQ.

Thinking Fast and Slow by Daniel Kahneman

One of the best books written on the workings and inherent biases of the human mind *Thinking Fast and Slow* takes its readers through distinct systems, System 1 and 2, that govern our decision-making process. The author, an eminent economist, takes the readers through potential psychological biases and how they can be minimized to derive personal and professional happiness. The best anecdote I remember from the book is that a group of monkeys made more money while picking stocks than Ivy League educated finance professionals. Ouch, that should really hurt.

If you want to read more books on behavioural psychology, I highly recommend *Nudge* and *Misbehaving* by Richard Thaler.

Sapiens by Yuval Noah Harari

Sapiens provides an incredible history of the world and an unbelievable journey from unsuspecting apes to the modern-day scientific marvels. Although it is not a business book, it provides incredible insights on driving a business through the power of a shared purpose, storytelling led abstract notions and what it takes to survive and thrive in any generation.

In conclusion, I hope I will rewrite this chapter again in the next print run of this book. Right now, the pending business books in my reading shelf include Steve Jobs' biography, *Billion Dollar Whale* (The man who fooled Wall Street and Hollywood) and *Homo Deus* (The history of tomorrow).

58

FOLLOWING A TRUE CALLING, NOT A FAKE HOBBY

As per the latest research by global gurus, passion has emerged necessary for daily subsistence. An extension of this Biblical gospel is the emergence of a hobby as the central tenet for human survival. In biological terms, hobby is the new kidney. You need a couple for proper survival.[78]

This chapter looks at the rise in the number of people trying to manufacture a fake kidney, sorry a fake hobby. In case you are feeling miserable about your life, read on for the following signals to identify a 'genuine fake'.

The DSLR Addict

The most common group of hobbyists are 'the DSLR addicts' who try to find natural beauty in everything, ranging from domesticated cockroaches to pig poop. This is followed up by a 300-word commentary on each picture on Instagram and personalized messages on WhatsApp. While this is bearable, it becomes creepy when 'the DSLR addict' starts taking pictures of young women in the name of candid camera salivating 'such a *pataka*'. Creep alert.

The Metrosexual Farmer

After decades of struggling in cities, the countryside and farming seems to be making a comeback. Getting closer to mother nature is the epitome for this breed of hobbyists. Their social media feeds are filled up with pictures of cute puppies in clean looking agrarian fields with tags comprising of natural, organic, green, clean, fulfilment amidst other passion-dosed phrases. Some of them are often caught trying to spot potato on the plant stem and *gur* (jaggery) on sugarcane. Wonder where the North Indian heat, the pesticides, the buffalos and the ugly tractors went?

The Palika Bazaar of Cult Fit

Do you have a friend who always poses with medals of having finished half marathons? Their captions tend to hover around, 'finished this race in record time' accompanied with a dozen selfies during the race. Quick question, 'how did you manage to finish your race in record time and manage to take so many selfies during that time?' Also, why aren't you physically active on the remaining 364 days as indicated by your generous flab. A sister profile of this breed is the fake yoga guru. Beware.

The Great Lover of Poverty

After the rise in Xiaomi phones, philanthropy has really taken off. Everyone seems to be waking up nights trying to rake up ways to help undernourished children in sub-Saharan Africa. This breed of hobbyists love to give back to society and hence start social media pages to garner donations for their funds. On a different note, did someone ask for a recommendation for philanthropic work for admission into an American business school? Such a kind-hearted soul.

The Nation Builder

This group of nation builders can be summarized in a single neat sentence, 'my leader is more virile than yours'.

This group of hobbyists can be characterized by excessive vitriolic, sorry passionate discussions on social media about their political leaders and their resultant nation building. This street fight multiplies disproportionately as seemingly sensible people start fighting like your mother and wife.

The Adventure Junkie

Mankind has seen a massive adrenaline shift after the birth of Instagram. In terms of importance, the birth of Instagram has been chronicled in the annals of history along with the extinction of dinosaurs, the invention of the steam engine and the Second World War. Adventures like rock climbing, paragliding, rafting, bungee jumping, sky diving are so yesterday. The adventure junkie is always looking for the next high. The next in-thing on their list is to spend a night inside a coffin with a skeleton. Apparently, the Google Pixel phone takes excellent low light pictures.

The Motivator

As you might be aware, India has fared very low on the happiness index. This has led to the birth of 'the motivator' whose single biggest mission is to make people realise their inner potential. To clarify, this is not the group of hobbyists that posts 'Good Morning,' 'I love you' and 'thank you' on all the family WhatsApp groups. The motivator genuinely believes in making people realize their potential, hence their social media feeds are filled up with, 'you can achieve', 'aim for the stars', 'follow your dreams', 'when the going gets tough, you get going' amidst other noble lines. As I write this, tears of gratitude are dripping down my face.

The Serial Entrepreneur

Once seen as a huge deal breaker in securing matrimonial alliances, the tag of an entrepreneur has come a long way. In common parlance, throw a stone at someone on 100-feet road in Bangalore and you will spot a visionary entrepreneur. This group of hobbyists who are under the inner torrential frenzy of adding value to everyone are obsessed with changing the world and making humanity a better place! I am sorry, how many of your start-ups have ever made a quarter of a penny in life?

The Cat Lover

A cat has nine lives and hence it lands up on the ninth spot on this list. Once upon a time, cute pets were synonymous with the Vodafone pug. As the Indian economy has leapfrogged, cats seem to have taken centre-stage. Screaming out, 'kitty kitty kitty' at restaurants is perceived to be extremely cool. This group of hobbyists indulges in putting up scintillating pictures of cat love, the success of their cats in a cat grooming race and pictures of cat manicure and pedicure. Please don't bark back at them in retaliation.

The Real Warren Buffett

It is ironical that Warren Buffett made so much money while this group of hobbyists barely get any publicity. This group is characterized by their know-it-all commentary on interest rates, stock market movement, hot picks, cool tips, lukewarm opportunities at dinner tables. It is unfortunate no one has ever asked them, 'mate, how much money have you made on your own?'

There are many more such passionate group of hobbyists, the enthusiastic historian, the artistic cake baker, the vintage dancer, the pseudo-intellectual educationist, the always right tarot card reader and so on. However, you should be careful while spilling your passion over to your immediate world. You don't want your social circles to go, 'fake hobby alert'.

In conclusion, for each of the above fake hobbies, there is always someone who is genuinely interested and enjoys doing a version of it, whether it is photography, nurturing pets, yoga, investing their own money in the capital markets or being a keen adventure sports lover. As long as they enjoy it and it helps them lead a better life, it is a great aspect of life to pursue. In fact, a very successful side hobby will often lead to the primary career showing more promise due to the synergistic effect of skills learnt from a well-pursued side hobby. If it is being done for Instagram or Snapchat only, that person should look at himself in the mirror very carefully!

59

STRESS FREE AND PRODUCTIVE IN TIMES OF A GLOBAL CRISIS

Working from home during this lockdown period seems to have increased work pressure and mental stress. This chapter looks at overcoming both during these unconventional times.[79]

Although most employees will not admit, 'work from home' has always been seen as a good thing. It typically involves more sleep, less working hours, an easy paced schedule and home-cooked food. However, with the current lockdown and the subsequent expectation of 'work from home' becoming the norm, employees have been reporting increasing stress due to the continued 'work from home' operating environment.

In this current environment with limited domestic help, 'work from home' involves participating in household chores. Every day seems like a working day with people conveniently forgetting boundaries between weekdays and weekends. Needless to say, the calls are getting longer and deeper into the night. Indian bosses are always under the wild trepidation imagining that their subordinates are sleeping throughout the day. Given this period of extra professional stress and no social relievers or physical activity, this chapter looks at simple hacks to make the soul crushing environment a tad more bearable.

Convince Yourself That 'Work from Home' Definitely Saves on Time!

Irrespective of what you might think, 'working from home' can save up to 20 hours every week. You read that correctly! A majority of the savings is in commute time. In a city like Bangalore, one of the worlds most congested cities, any commute beyond 5 km is at least an hour affair with another 30 minutes with cab cancellations and inability to locate places due to poor networks and call drops. Add an early morning or a late-night flight every other week and you are saving an extra five hours in transit and travel time. Without any outdoor socializing with your boss, nearly one or two evenings in a week are completely spared. Add up all of this and you make a neat four extra hours every day. Pure extra time!

A Boring Routine Is the Key to Beat the Blues!

The problem of excessive stress might get aggravated if someone decides to get up late, have a hearty breakfast, start the day at 11 AM, take a de-stressing shower post lunch, prepare a long home-cooked meal and then panic because of the insurmountable work that gets added by the evening.

A fixed routine of getting up and being ready for work by 8:30 AM will go a long way in making the day bearable. Psychological hacks to having a clean, spacious and well-lit desk will make the working environment pleasant. In addition, it will help to eat home cooked meals on time. Also, follow the Japanese principle of eating only till 80 per cent of your hunger is satiated. The last thing your company needs is a bunch of pumpkins working for them.

While a disciplined routine might sound difficult, it can prove to be highly beneficial. A fixed 30-minute nap in the afternoon can greatly aid productivity. In addition, sleeping at a fixed time every day can also help in making up for months of sleep deficit!

The Key to Succeeding Is Tuning Your Mind to Change!

Given every day is 'work from home', the expectations from work are bound to change. Weekends will no longer be sacrosanct, welcome to working with Indian bosses! This is a reality that should be accepted in most professional service firms. However, there will be a certain amount of downtime during the week. After all, there is only so much useless work that can be created when the entire economy has come to a standstill. The mind should be tuned to this change and can be persuaded to pick up a new hobby—reading the newspaper, progressing on your reading lists, picking up an old hobby. It is also the perfect time to kick the butt and reduce dependence on alcohol and wine. Not to mention throwing away old clothes and shoes and giving your room a new look altogether.

Run Baby Run!

Staying indoors perennially can be depressing to say the least. In such a scenario, regular physical activity and absorbing sunlight can prove to be therapeutic. While we are all homebound, physical activity can range from home exercises, good old use of the skipping rope, a few stretches to get that extra adipose in shape or yoga in the apartment terrace. Walking while speaking numerous hours on the phone can be hugely beneficial. It is also a good time to indulge in household chores, buying vegetables and cleaning the toilets. It makes sense to do it with care and enthusiasm as you might turn out to be more endearing at home and as a result, less frustrated.

Disconnect Away from Digital Toxin!

Most of us spend nearly three to five hours on our smartphones everyday browsing carelessly. This idle time can be productively used by reducing non-value add transactions. Avoid reading the same news again and again every few hours. The news is depressing and there is little novelty about the situation. With the barrage of fake articles being circulated (e.g., post this picture on the pages of five Facebook friends and coronavirus will never enter your doorstep), it is prudent to switch off family WhatsApp groups. The purest form of digital toxin to be avoided at this point is the 'my leader is better than your leader' debate on social media. In case you find someone repeatedly posting toxin along the above lines, snooze that person for some time. Keep yourself happy by posting pictures of yourself reading, cooking (e.g., making the Dalgona coffee), skipping or even making your bed. Finally, it is best to avoid speculating on the future. Digital discussions on 'what will happen next month, when the economy will come back, when will we go back to office' are futile and emotionally draining. This extra time saved can be used for all the other items mentioned earlier.

Make Less Shallow Digital Connections!

The importance of bitching on an everyday basis when the world is going around in circles can never be underestimated. A 15-minute bitching call with your office colleagues to pour your hearts out, typically against your bosses, is a very practical idea to stay connected. In case you think the suggestion is trivial, please google the term, 'commercial benefits of office gossip'. Given the downtime, it is also a great idea to connect with old friends over weekends and reminiscence over enjoyable moments in the past.

In conclusion, we are going through an unfortunate time that occurs once in many decades. While a recurring 'working from home' environment might seem more stressful than working regularly in office, following some of the above hacks might make this period a tad more bearable.

60 LEARNINGS FROM A TREK UP TO TIGER'S NEST

Climbing mountains have known to have a therapeutic effect on the human body and the soul.[80] Mountains often represent the microcosm of life and the journey of an individual through his life. I had the privilege of recently trekking up the toughest 160 floors in my life, to pay homage to Guru Padmasambhava in Tiger's Nest, Paro, Bhutan.

Tiger's Nest is a small monastery hung on a cliff over-looking a spectacular valley. It is one of the most majestic tourist attractions in this part of the world. The legend goes that *Guru Padmasambhava* flew on the back of a tigress, hence the name, to tame the local devil. He then meditated at one of the caves for many years and so the place became holy. He has been credited to have brought Buddhism to Bhutan.

Following are some of the career lessons which the gorgeous mountains wanted me to mull over.

The Journey Is Worth More than the Destination

The beauty of Tiger's Nest is the journey till the summit, comprising the breath-taking views, the ad hoc difficulties encountered while trekking up, the internal resilience required to make it to the apex. While the visit to the set of eight temples is rewarding, the reward is amplified due to the quality of the journey undertaken to get there.

A corporate career is rarely about the title or the compensation at the end of a three-decade long career. It is often about the choices made to get there, undertaking difficult but enriching assignments, working with supportive colleagues and mentors, building necessary capabilities and garnering requisite experiences. It is a gamut of these aspects that make the end state worth it.

Hard Work and Preparation, in the Right Amount, Is the Key

It is necessary to be in the appropriate physical condition before commencing on a difficult trek. Moderate regular physical activity, suitable diet before the trek and a well-rested body are essential before embarking on the journey. It is also necessary to read up on the details of the trek to be mentally prepared for what is in store ahead.

The right amount of preparation is the key in any corporate engagement. The critical word is 'right' and not 'relentless'. You do not want to be underprepared at any part of the journey but you do not want to be overburdened and exhausted before the assignment has even begun. A burnout is rarely desirable at any stage of your corporate career.

You Are Only Competing with Yourself

While you are trekking up Tiger's Nest, you will see tourists pursuing the journey at their own pace without worrying about time taken by them or their neighbour. In fact, you will notice random tourists helping each other with food, water or a helping hand over a difficult ridge. You will notice that people rarely post their 'time to ascend' on social media too as there is no point posting given it is not a competition.

This behaviour should be symptomatic about life in general as every individual is only competing with himself or herself during a three-decade long career. Career movements and salaries of neighbouring colleagues should rarely matter.

In fact, what matters is lending them a helping hand at times. It is bound to come back in a good way.

Don't Give Up, Take a Break but Don't Give Up

The trek equivalent of 160 floors to 10,000 feet above sea level amidst occasional showers, low single digit temperatures and treacherous pathways can be difficult for the fittest of people. There are many tourists who give up the trek midway and return to base camp as they are convinced they won't be able to pursue the road ahead. I feel it is a 'state of mind' that forces people to quit. Had they rested for a few minutes and gone ahead, they wouldn't have missed out on the fantastic journey.

Similarly, in a corporate career, during a difficult business environment, the words 'I quit' should be the last ones said or actually not said at all. Often, a short break to divert the inner trappings of the mind can be enough to recharge a person for the difficult but rewarding journey ahead.

Expect the Unexpected to Happen

A trek up till Tiger's Nest is often difficult for the fittest of people and can rarely be planned on an excel sheet. There are aspects that are bound to go wrong. An ad hoc shower, a slippery and potentially dangerous trail, physical fatigue, a mule heading down towards you with passion, losing your way are some of the unexpected events that can happen while ascending or descending Tiger's Nest. Rather than fretting over these and losing your mind, it is essential to calmly overcome these mini obstacles.

In a professional career, despite the best of intentions and planning, unexpected things do and often happen. A change in boss, fluctuating company fortunes, an unreasonable client, an irate junior, a key member of the team quitting are events that should be expected in day-to-day business and carefully handled without losing one's cool.

Appreciate the Power of Silence

Besides the fatigue and the breath-taking views that accompany you as you trek up the mountain, the one thing that is truly appreciative is the power of silence. The silence is only natural as Tiger's Nest owes its existence to a guru who visited the place to meditate and achieve his inner objectives. Like they keep saying in the *Kung Fu Panda* series, silence can lead to 'inner peace'.

In our daily lives which are flooded with social media distractions, fake news, artificial political associations, the pressure of 'keeping up with the Joneses' and barrage of office politics, the power of silence and meditation can be therapeutic for the mind and the soul besides drastically improving the quality of one's life.

You Are Not the Centre of the Universe

A trek up equivalent to 160 floors flanked by a breath-taking valley, spectacular views of the fog making the temples visible and hidden at the same time along with monasteries resting on a treacherous cliff 10,000 feet above the sea level can be humbling for any human being no matter his/her personal achievements. The grandeur of nature amidst the calmness and serene environment is bound to make any person deeply humble and respectful.

In case of individuals holding the deep belief that the world is centred around them, the natural majesty is bound to make everyone think twice about the inflated value attributed to his/her professional importance.

Conquer Your Fears

The trek to the top of the hill is treacherous and difficult. Besides the high altitude and the physical difficulty involved, the path uphill can be slippery and dangerous during certain times of the year. Despite this, you will see millions of tourists every year conquer their fears and make it to the site of the holy pilgrimage to get a view of the breath-taking monastery.

A long career is a combination of undertaking roles and assignments that are difficult, outside your comfort zone and downright risky. Besides the difficulty of the unknown, they also involve conquering your internal demons to take up something that can be enriching and rewarding in the future.

In conclusion, a mountain trek teaches you many things that are representative about life. The physical and mental exercise results in a deep understanding of an all-encompassing nature and the humility we all feel at the sight of these gorgeous creations. I strongly recommend a trek every year to nourish the soul and bring out the necessary perspective in every person's life.

Food for Thought

As we come to the end of this chapter, I am writing down some of the most interesting interview questions I have asked or have come across. Take up these and see how you would approach them. There is no right answer, hence I am not prescribing a solution. However, I will provide some directional guidelines.

You are an advisor to Shah Rukh Khan on his career path. What do you think he should do over the next 3, 5 and 10 years?

The key question is to evaluate how much can he succeed in movies from here on, basis the historical past. Should he change the scripts he is choosing? Should he look at adjacent media leveraging his strengths of good speech and wit in television and web series? Should he enter an adjacent industry like web series production? Should he enter industries where he can leverage his brand name like fashion, food or hospitality?

61

FINALLY: 10 COMMANDMENTS TO LEADING A MEANINGFUL LIFE!

As we come to the last chapter in this book, I think it will be of help to you to make a personal charter which you can leverage going forward. Following the commandments below is bound to improve your quality of professional and personal life. I will admit none of these commandments are rocket science, they are common sensical which you are already aware of. However, most things in life are fairly simple which we don't end up following. Having a simple charter documented in two pages and ready for future reference might be a little bit more effective to help you live it. I would strongly suggest you write your individual goals against each of these commandments which you want to achieve over the next 3, 6 and 12 months and revisit those after that.

Pursue a Hobby Relentlessly

A corporate job, while is absolutely necessary for financial and social sustenance, can be miserable for the soul. It is absolutely necessary to build an alternate career, something which you like. It will aid in increasing your self-esteem and personal identity beyond the company you work for and help bring in inner joy. A hobby can be absolutely anything—photography, writing, playing an instrument, running, teaching. I would strongly suggest you actively post your progress on social media so that the world knows about it, the dopamine kick your body will keep getting will encourage you on to do more and feel good about yourself.

Block People on Social Media Who Make You Unhappy

Most misery in everyday millennial lives are caused by tracking others on social media, an over-achiever, someone with an alternate political opinion or an irritating acquaintance. There is an easy solution, please ignore them on social media by ensuring their posts don't pollute your feeds. If you are feeling bad about yourself someday, go and read the social media page of someone whom you know is surely doing worse off than you. You will be amazed at how much of a mood lifter it is. Also, please stay off social media consciously for one day a week, at least.

Nature Is the Biggest Enricher of the Human Soul

There are few things that are more therapeutic in life than jogging in an open park or climbing a mountain. People who are fit physically are fit mentally. There is absolutely no excuse to not undertake physical activity. A simple starting point should be 10,000 steps a day for at least four days every week. As I have highlighted earlier, a yearly mountain trek is highly recommended for its impact in healing a tired soul. And please go ahead and post it on social media to make your friends die of envy.

Relationships, Social and Personal, Are More in the Moment and Evolve Regularly

The nature of relationships, social and personal, are changing in contemporary times. They are not as long lasting and geographically close as they used to be. Individuals are changing faster, moving more often, meeting different people regularly and expecting more from life every day. Hence, it is imperative that people don't get too attached to relationships, personal and social. These are transient by definition and everyone should be prepared to move on. What stays permanent is individual family which should be given due importance.

Avoid Unnecessary Conflicts

One of my mentors would always advise, 'Always stand up during a fight. The best fights, however, are the ones that are never fought'. It is absolutely practical to tread on a conflict avoidance path, at office, with the local cab driver or on social media. It is stupid, if not immature, to fight with friends over social media over some political leader's comments. Any fight takes a lot out of anyone, physically and emotionally. Unless the world is coming to an end, it is just not worth it. Look no further than Mahendra Singh Dhoni.

Enrich Yourself By Reading a Book and Watching a Web Series Every Month

Learning is an ongoing process till the final day of your life. Self-learning brings inner joy, besides making you more competent at work and in life. The most enjoyable avenues for learning in life are reading and watching very good web series. It is a good idea to read at least one book a month and finish one web series a month. Given that I am the author of this book, I am going to promote my work shamelessly. Please start by reading my other books, *Yours Sarcastically* and *Satan's Angels*.

Sleep Like a Baby

Lack of quality sleep is the most underrated pain point of modern life. Deprived sleep leads to a tired body leading to a tired mind ending in a miserable day at work accelerating towards a miserable life. Sleep should be the most important priority for anyone, an eight-hour uninterrupted sleep cycle. A disciplined sleep routine will aid in healing your body and making you feel good about yourselves.

Get a Second Phone

With our digitally active lives encroaching into our personal space and with corporate expectations of being available 24×7, it is practical to get a second phone, the number to which is available only with a few select friends and family. And be unapologetic to switch off your main phone on weekends and after 9 PM on a weekday. Your mental peace is in your SIM cards.

Give Away a Small Portion of Your Time to Charity

It has been scientifically proven that there are few joys in life greater than assisting others in succeeding. A bit of time invested in helping an office intern, teaching at a local school or helping someone make a résumé can go a long way in building up good karma and having a less hollow view to life in general.

There are nine commandments I have written about so far. The tenth commandment, possibly the most important one, is to forgive yourself. There is no point in harbouring regrets, for a poor grade, a failed relationship, a missed office promotion, a failed examination or a personal mishap. It is never too late to start afresh in life, never.

In conclusion, I would like to genuinely thank you for taking your time out and investing it in my book. I hope you have enjoyed this conversation and can take back a lot more to your life.

Also, like any good book series, this one will have a sequel. Don't forget to pick that one too:)

Thanks again!

NOTES

1. My two other books are titled *Yours Sarcastically* and *Satan's Angels*.

2. Adapted from a similar article by the author for *Businessworld*. For the entire list of author articles, please visit http://www.businessworld.in/author/Guest-Author/Sandeep-Das-82696/

3. Adapted from a similar article by the author for *Businessworld*. For the entire list of author articles, please visit http://www.businessworld.in/author/Guest-Author/Sandeep-Das-82696/

4. As consumption is 60 per cent of our GDP, you always hear news narratives on why domestic demand (aka consumption) is imperative for our economy, https://economictimes.indiatimes.com/news/economy/indicators/indias-worrying-growth-statistics-and-what-they-mean-for-the-future/articleshow/72735008.cms

5. For a more nuanced view, visit http://statisticstimes.com/economy/sectorwise-gdp-contribution-of-india.php or the site of the (you guessed it) government of India

6. I always visit Investopedia for understanding economics concepts and procuring related information. In case you want to further understand the size of each of the major global economies, please visit https://www.investopedia.com/insights/worlds-top-economies/

7. For the nerds, if you are looking to understand the 100-year inflation trend in India, please visit https://www.statista.com/statistics/271322/inflation-rate-in-india/

8. Did you think it was a printing mistake? (https://uk.reuters.com/article/us-venezuela-economy/venezuela-inflation-454-percent-in-first-quarter-national-assembly-idUKKBN1HI2MO)

9. To get a clearer movie on the lost decade for Japan (the 1990s) where it faced economic stagnation and price deflation (https://www.investopedia.com/articles/economics/08/japan-1990s-credit-crunch-liquidity-trap.asp)

10. This is the link to the original article: https://hbr.org/1979/03/how-competitive-forces-shape-strategy

11. This fascinating story is explained in great detail in the book and the movie titled *Barbarians at the Gate*.

12. In case you get a kick out of such large transactions of money, you may read https://www.blackstone.com/the-firm/press-releases/article/hilton-hotels-corporation-to-be-acquired-by-black stone-investments-funds

13. Adapted from a similar article by the author for *Businessworld*. For the entire list of author articles, please visit http://www.businessworld.in/author/Guest-Author/Sandeep-Das-82696/

14. Here is a link to the book: http://www.build-borrow-buy.com/laurence-capron/?LMCL=fDePuC. I strongly recommend you read this book.

15. Adapted from a similar article by the author for *Businessworld*. For the entire list of author articles, please visit http://www.businessworld.in/author/Guest-Author/Sandeep-Das-82696/

16. Adapted from a similar article by the author for *Businessworld*. For the entire list of author articles, please visit http://www.businessworld.in/author/Guest-Author/Sandeep-Das-82696/

17. To get a good perspective on the numerous rounds of financing Flipkart has witnessed, please visit https://www.financialexpress.com/industry/technology/the-flipkart-story-a-timeline-of-funding-from-2007-to-2017/595740/

18. Adapted from a similar article by the author for *Businessworld*. For the entire list of author articles, please visit http://www.businessworld.in/author/Guest-Author/Sandeep-Das-82696/

19. https://www.forbes.com/sites/neilpatel/2015/01/16/90-of-startups-will-fail-heres-what-you-need-to-know-about-the-10/#aae15e667926

20. Adapted from a similar article by the author for *Businessworld*. For the entire list of author articles, please visit http://www.businessworld.in/author/Guest-Author/Sandeep-Das-82696/

21. Adapted from a similar article by the author for *Businessworld*. For the entire list of author articles, please visit http://www.businessworld.in/author/Guest-Author/Sandeep-Das-82696/

22. Adapted from a similar article by the author for *Businessworld*. For the entire list of author articles, please visit http://www.businessworld.in/author/Guest-Author/Sandeep-Das-82696/

23. Here is an article on the likely evolution of the grocery channel: http://www.businessworld.in/article/Future-Of-The-Local-Kirana-Is-Destined-To-Be-Bright/14-05-2020-192083/

24. Here is a column on the controversial protests against food delivery companies like Zomato: https://theprint.in/economy/how-zomato-went-from-food-industry-fairytale-to-evil-corporation/279592/

25. Interestingly, for e-commerce, consumer electronics, fashion and mobile phones nearly constitute 65 per cent of their sales: https://economictimes.indiatimes.com/industry/services/retail/right-click-the-ecommerce-disaster-that-never-was/articleshow/69967082.cms?from=mdr

26. TikTok has in excess of 200 million users in India compared to Facebook at about 300 million users. Are you on TikTok? Please visit for an understanding of active users: https://economictimes.indiatimes.com/small-biz/startups/features/bytedance-bets-big-on-short-videos-to-engage-indian-market-takes-on-facebook/articleshow/69422493.cms?from=mdr

27. Rural India is the holy grail of Indian FMCGs. While it constitutes 40 per cent of their business, it adds significant operational complexity to reach the rural consumer. For a view on these numbers, please visit - https://www.livemint.com/industry/retail/in-rural-india-smaller-packs-gain-favour-as-incomes-shrink-11581622202600.html

NOTES

28.   Adapted from a similar article by the author for *Businessworld*. For the entire list of author articles, please visit http://www.businessworld.in/author/Guest-Author/Sandeep-Das-82696/

29.   Adapted from a similar article by the author for *Businessworld*. For the entire list of author articles, please visit http://www.businessworld.in/author/Guest-Author/Sandeep-Das-82696/

30.   You can feel nice or miserable, depending on which country you are in. http://economics.mit.edu/files/3230 (France's 35-hour week), https://www.news18.com/news/buzz/germany-bans-managers-from-calling-or-emailing-staff-after-work-hours-677249.html, https://www.nytimes.com/2016/05/21/business/international/in-sweden-an-experiment-turns-shorter-workdays-into-bigger-gains.html

31.   Adapted from a similar article by the author for *Businessworld*. For the entire list of author articles, please visit http://www.businessworld.in/author/Guest-Author/Sandeep-Das-82696/

32.   Adapted from a similar article by the author for MensXP *Times of India*. For the entire list of author articles, please visit https://www.mensxp.com/author/507-sandeep-das.html

33.   Here is a link to some more gory details, https://www.history.com/topics/great-depression/great-depression-history

34.   In case you want to feel worse about the crisis, https://www.investopedia.com/terms/a/asian-financial-crisis.asp

35.   Some of you would have been in your nappies during this time, https://www.investopedia.com/terms/d/dotcom-bubble.asp

36.   You can either watch the movie *The Big Short* or read the book that inspired the movie, https://www.amazon.com/Big-Short-Inside-Doomsday-Machine/dp/0393338827

37.   https://economictimes.indiatimes.com/news/economy/policy/4-reforms-that-pulled-india-back-after-it-ran-out-of-money-in-1991/articleshow/53308703.cms?from=mdr

38. Adapted from a similar article by the author for *Businessworld*. For the entire list of author articles, please visit http://www.businessworld.in/author/Guest-Author/Sandeep-Das-82696/

39. Adapted from a similar article by the author for *Businessworld*. For the entire list of author articles, please visit http://www.businessworld.in/author/Guest-Author/Sandeep-Das-82696/

40. Basis my discussions with various FMCG industry leaders.

41. Adapted from a similar article by the author for *Businessworld*. For the entire list of author articles, please visit http://www.businessworld.in/author/Guest-Author/Sandeep-Das-82696/

42. Minimalism has its sources in Buddhism. To get a view on deploying these at the workplace, you can also look at https://www.forbes.com/sites/drewhansen/2016/12/27/minimalism-documentary-netflix-career-principles/#3a527f87706b

43. Adapted from a similar article by the author for *Businessworld*. For the entire list of author articles, please visit http://www.businessworld.in/author/Guest-Author/Sandeep-Das-82696/

44. Adapted from a similar article by the author for *Businessworld*. For the entire list of author articles, please visit http://www.businessworld.in/author/Guest-Author/Sandeep-Das-82696/

45. A highly recommended YouTube channel. He speaks of the interaction among chemicals in this video - https://www.youtube.com/watch?v=lmyZMtPVodo

46. Adapted from a similar article by the author for *Businessworld*. For the entire list of author articles, please visit http://www.businessworld.in/author/Guest-Author/Sandeep-Das-82696/

47. https://brandequity.economictimes.indiatimes.com/news/marketing/jk-super-cement-ups-marketing-spend-by-50/71798929

48. https://www.livemint.com/Money/i0RDJSc2PWJohiqt 1ZoKoM/Cement-cos-devise-ways-to-save-on-freight-costs. html

49. Adapted from a similar article by the author for *Businessworld*. For the entire list of author articles, please visit http://www. businessworld.in/author/Guest-Author/Sandeep-Das-82696/

50. Adapted from a similar article by the author for *Businessworld*. For the entire list of author articles, please visit http://www. businessworld.in/author/Guest-Author/Sandeep-Das-82696/

51. Adapted from a similar article by the author for *Businessworld*. For the entire list of author articles, please visit http://www. businessworld.in/author/Guest-Author/Sandeep-Das-82696/

52. Adapted from a similar article by the author for *Businessworld*. For the entire list of author articles, please visit http://www. businessworld.in/author/Guest-Author/Sandeep-Das-82696/

53. Adapted from a similar article by the author for Outlook Money. For the entire list of author articles, please visit https:// www.outlookindia.com/outlookmoney/author/sandeep-das

54. Adapted from a similar article by the author for *Businessworld*. For the entire list of author articles, please visit http://www. businessworld.in/author/Guest-Author/Sandeep-Das-82696/

55. For a more detailed understanding of the Indian FMCG industry, you can start with the following link https://www. ibef.org/industry/Fmcg-presentation

56. In rural India, how small packs are increasingly gaining traction: https://www.livemint.com/industry/retail/in-rural-india-smaller-packs-gain-favour-as-incomes-shrink-1158162220 2600.html

57. For an excellent overview of Unilever's strategy and dividing Indian into multiple mini Indias, please read https://www. businesstoday.in/magazine/indias-most-valuable-companies-2018/on-a-winning-streak/story/286844.html

58. Read for a view on the number of active local *kirana* outlets: https://www.livemint.com/industry/retail/the-neighbourhood

-kirana-store-makes-a-roaring-comeback-this-season-11586
545799321.html

59. Read for a view on how the channel contributions of general trade, modern trade and e-commerce are evolving in India: https:// www.livemint.com/industry/retail/organized-retail-now-account-for-30-of-fmcg-sales-in-metro-cities-nielsen-11588 256571543.html

60. Read this point of view for a view on the evolving e-commerce landscape in India: https://www.pwc.in/research-insights/2018/ propelling-india-towards-global-leadership-in-e-commerce. html

61. Read for an interesting view on likely trends in e-commerce in India: https://retail.economictimes.indiatimes.com/news/e-commerce/e-tailing/trends-to-watch-out-for-in-the-e-commerce-sector-2020/73422007

62. Read for an interesting view on how Tier 1 and 2 towns are going online: https://yourstory.com/2019/08/startup-bharat-consumers-tier-ii-iii-cities-ecommerce-food-delivery

63. Sometimes the wiki page gives a very good view on what happened. Here is the link to understand the 'Occupy Wall Street Movement' - https://en.wikipedia.org/wiki/Occupy_Wall_Street

64. Read for understanding the journey of the Pradhan Mantri Jan-Dhan Yojana:- https://pmjdy.gov.in

65. For the numerically inclined, this article comprises a set of numbers—https://timesofindia.indiatimes.com/business/ india-business/credit-has-to-expand-18-20-for-india-to-become-5tn-eco/articleshow/70745427.cms

66. To get a better understanding of this data, you can visit the website of the Ministry of Finance, Government of India.

67. To get a better understanding of this data, you can visit the website of the Ministry of Finance, Government of India.

68. Adapted from a similar article by the author for *Businessworld*. For the entire list of author articles, please visit http://www. businessworld.in/author/Guest-Author/Sandeep-Das-82696/

69. Adapted from a similar article by the author for *Businessworld*. For the entire list of author articles, please visit http://www. businessworld.in/author/Guest-Author/Sandeep-Das-82696/

70. Adapted from a similar article by the author for *Businessworld*. For the entire list of author articles, please visit http://www. businessworld.in/author/Guest-Author/Sandeep-Das-82696/

71. Adapted from a similar article by the author for *Businessworld*. For the entire list of author articles, please visit http://www. businessworld.in/author/Guest-Author/Sandeep-Das-82696/

72. Adapted from a similar article by the author for *Businessworld*. For the entire list of author articles, please visit http://www. businessworld.in/author/Guest-Author/Sandeep-Das-82696/

73. Adapted from a similar article by the author for Businessworld. For the entire list of author articles, please visit http://www. businessworld.in/author/Guest-Author/Sandeep-Das-82696/

74. Adapted from a similar article by the author for Businessworld. For the entire list of author articles, please visit http://www. businessworld.in/author/Guest-Author/Sandeep-Das-82696/

75. Adapted from a similar article by the author for Businessworld. For the entire list of author articles, please visit http://www. businessworld.in/author/Guest-Author/Sandeep-Das-82696/

76. Adapted from a similar article by the author for *Businessworld*. For the entire list of author articles, please visit http://www. businessworld.in/author/Guest-Author/Sandeep-Das-82696/

77. Adapted from a similar article by the author for MensXP— *Times of India*. For the entire list of author articles, please visit https://www.mensxp.com/author/507-sandeep-das.html

78. Adapted from a similar article by the author for Mens XP—*Times of India*. For the entire list of author articles, please visit https://www.mensxp.com/author/507-sandeep-das.html

79. Adapted from a similar article by the author for Businessworld. For the entire list of author articles, please visit http://www. businessworld.in/author/Guest-Author/Sandeep-Das-82696/

80. Adapted from a similar article by the author for *Businessworld*. For the entire list of author articles, please visit http://www. businessworld.in/author/Guest-Author/Sandeep-Das-82696/

NOTES